Special Education Programs

The Program Evaluation Guides for Schools
Richard M. Jaeger, Series Editor

Evaluating School Programs: An Educator's Guide
James R. Sanders

Special Education Programs: A Guide to Evaluation
Ada L. Vallecorsa, Laurie U. deBettencourt, Elizabeth Garriss

Counseling Programs: A Guide to Evaluation
L. DiAnne Borders, Sandra M. Drury

Reading and Language Arts Programs: A Guide to Evaluation
Mary W. Olson, Samuel D. Miller

Programs for At-Risk Students: A Guide to Evlauation
Rita G. O'Sullivan, Cheryl V. Tennant

Mathematics Programs: A Guide to Evaluation
George W. Bright, A. Edward Uprichard, Janice H. Jetton

Ada L. Vallecorsa
Laurie U. deBettencourt
Elizabeth Garriss

Special Education Programs
A Guide to Evaluation

The Program Evaluation Guides for Schools
Series Editor: Richard M. Jaeger

CORWIN PRESS, INC.
A Sage Publications Company
Newbury Park, California 91320

Copyright © 1992 by Corwin Press, Inc.

All rights reserved. No part of this book may be reproduced or utilized in any form or by any means, electronic or mechanical, including photocopying, recording, or by any information storage and retrieval system, without permission in writing from the publisher.

For information address:

Corwin Press, Inc.
A Sage Publications Company
2455 Teller Road
Newbury Park, California 91320

SAGE Publications Ltd.
6 Bonhill Street
London EC2A 4PU
United Kingdom

SAGE Publications India Pvt. Ltd.
M-32 Market
Greater Kailash I
New Delhi 110 048 India

Printed in the United States of America

Library of Congress Cataloging-in-Publication Data
Vallecorsa, Ada L., 1948-
    Special education programs : a guide to evaluation / Ada L. Vallecorsa, Laurie U. deBettencourt, Elizabeth Garriss.
        p.   cm.   —(Essential tools for educators)
    Includes bibliographical references (p.   ) and index.
    ISBN 0-8039-6034-4
    1. Handicapped children—Education—United States—Evaluation. 2. Special education—United States—Evaluation. I. deBettencourt, Laurie Ungerleider. II. Garriss, Elizabeth. III. Title
IV. Series.
LC4031.V27   1992
371.91—dc 20   92-26634

The paper in this book meets the specifications for permanence of the American National Standards Institute and the National Association of State Textbook Administrators.

92 93 94 95   10 9 8 7 6 5 4 3 2 1

Corwin Press Production Editor: Tara S. Mead

Contents

Series Editor's Preface vii

About the Authors ix

Introduction 1

Vignette One Teacher Needs for Staff Development 11

Vignette Two Appropriateness of Least Restrictive 20
Environment (LRE) Placements

Vignette Three Satisfaction of Program Participants 40

Vignette Four What's Going On in Classrooms? 52

Vignette Five What's in an Individualized 71
Educational Plan (IEP)?

Vignette Six Assessing the Generalization of Skills 83
to Other Settings

Conclusion 96

Resource A: Standards and Indicators 97
for Evaluation of Special Education Programs
With Suggested Evaluation Methods

Resource B: Selected References 105

Index 109

Series Editor's Preface

Essential Tools for Educators: The Program Evaluation Guides for Schools is a series grounded in the premise that regular evaluation of school programs can be of enormous help to school professionals—provided *they* are the ones who plan the evaluations, conduct the evaluations, and use the evaluations to guide their school improvement activities. Evaluation is a powerful tool for documenting school needs, identifying strengths and weaknesses in school programs, and discovering how to improve almost every aspect of school life. Program evaluation need not be complex or inordinately time consuming. Simple principles and strategies are described in the initial volume of this series, *Evaluating School Programs: An Educator's Guide*. Then, specific techniques and approaches are illustrated in the program-focused guides that complete the series. Using these principles and techniques, teachers, principals, and other school professionals *can* plan, conduct, and interpret the findings of powerful evaluations of their curricula; of their instructional programs in mathematics, reading, language arts, and special education; of their programs for "at-risk" students; and of their counseling and personnel development programs. The principles to be learned from this series can be applied even more broadly to the evaluation of school disciplinary programs, student assessment programs, community relations programs, and other programmatic elements that are central to the successful functioning of a school.

Extensive technical training is *not* prerequisite to planning and conducting sound evaluations of school programs. Sound evaluation *does* require a desire to improve one's school, willingness to work collegially, careful attention to detail, and basic knowledge of how school program evaluations should be carried out. The ETE series provides school professionals with the last of these elements—the essential tools they need to plan and conduct effective evaluations of their school programs.

Evaluating School Programs: An Educator's Guide is the foundation volume in this series. It contains a clear, concise exposition of the objectives, principles, and core issues that undergird solid evaluations of school programs. By reading this guide, teachers, principals, and their colleagues will learn how to (a) determine the feasibility of conducting a school program evaluation, (b) focus a school program evaluation, (c) structure and design a school program evaluation, (d) conduct a school program evaluation, (e) interpret the results of a school program evaluation, (f) report and make use of the results of a school program evaluation, and (g) ensure that a school program evaluation is conducted ethically, damages no one, and enriches all who are associated with the program being evaluated.

Once these basic elements of a school evaluation are well understood, readers will be ready to proceed to the guide in this series that focuses on the subject area of the program to be evaluated. Each program-specific guide provides specific instruction on the evaluation of school programs in a single subject area, and each follows a consistent pattern of organization. Following an introduction that provides an overview and rationale for program evaluation in its subject area, each program-specific guide contains a sequence of vignettes that illustrate, in detail, evaluation of a focused aspect of a school program. Collectively, these vignettes illustrate how evaluations of school programs are planned, structured, staffed, conducted, interpreted, and used. The vignettes cover a wide range of practical evaluative issues; illustrate the selection, development, and use of a large number of evaluation strategies and instruments; and show how the results of evaluation can be used to strengthen school programs. Resources at the end of each program-specific guide contain a set of research-based standards and indicators of school program quality, a road map to the use of these standards in evaluating the effectiveness and efficiency of a school program, and an annotated bibliography of selected references on program evaluation in the subject area of the guide.

Evaluations can help school professionals make their school the best it can be and, in the process, substantially increase their own educational effectiveness. In the hands of thoughtful, well-trained school professionals, evaluation can be a transformative catalyst that improves schools and all who work and learn in them. The ETE series will help you become one of those distinctive school professionals who can make school program evaluations work well. Knowing that your investment in this knowledge will pay rich dividends for years to come, I wish you every success.

RICHARD M. JAEGER
*University of North Carolina,
Greensboro*

About the Authors

Ada L. Vallecorsa earned her doctoral degree in special education (with a particular emphasis in the area of learning disabilities) at the University of Pittsburgh. She also has advanced training in the areas of speech and language disorders and audiology. She was awarded a postdoctoral fellowship at the Learning Resource and Development Center at the University of Pittsburgh, where she participated in program evaluation studies in special education classrooms. She has had more than 10 years' experience in public school settings working as a speech therapist, hearing specialist, and resource-room teacher. Currently, she is an Associate Professor in the Department of Pedagogical Studies at the University of North Carolina at Greensboro, where she also serves as coordinator of the graduate program in special education. Her professional interests have centered around approaches to informal assessment in special education, development of literacy skills among students with learning disabilities, transition issues for secondary-level students with disabilities, and approaches to program evaluation in special education. For the past 10 years, she has also been involved in the development and evaluation of teacher preparation programs for students in both special and general education.

Laurie U. deBettencourt received her doctoral degree in special education from the University of Virginia in 1984. She completed a postdoctoral fellowship at the University of Pittsburgh in 1985. She is currently an Assistant Professor at the University of North Carolina at Greensboro in the Department of Pedagogical Studies. She has had 5 years' experience working in public and private school settings with students who have learning disabilities, emotional disabilities, and mild retardation. Her current research interests include teaching cognitive strategies to secondary students with mild disabilities, analyzing what happens to students with mild disabilities after high school, using curriculum-based measurement procedures with students with learning disabilities, and studying approaches to program evaluation in special education. She has published several articles in such journals as *Exceptional Children, Intervention in School and Clinic, Cognition and Instruction,* and *Teacher Education and Special Education.*

Elizabeth Garriss is a doctoral candidate at the University of North Carolina at Greensboro. Her area of focus is early childhood special education with emphasis on the education of preschool children with disabilities. Her research interests include the benefits of mainstreaming, social interaction among preschool children, and the benefits of family involvement in preschool education. Currently a teacher with the Greensboro public schools, she is involved with the development of assessment instruments for Chapter 1 prekindergarten programs. A strong proponent of mainstreaming young children, she includes in her professional concerns the design and implementation of quality integrated programs for preschool children with and without disabilities. An educator with 24 years' experience (regular classroom, resource, and administrative), she specializes in the education of young children with disabilities and those at risk for learning difficulties.

Introduction

Nowhere is the need for program evaluation more evident than in the field of special education. Since passage of P.L. 94-142, the Education of All Handicapped Children Act, program evaluation has been a required activity in special education to ensure that programs and projects are meeting their intended goals. Although early efforts in this regard focused almost exclusively on questions of legal compliance, more recent efforts have shifted to include many areas of interest. School personnel are now interested in questions that go beyond issues of program access and procedural safeguards. They increasingly are interested in addressing issues of program appropriateness and program quality. For example, it is no longer enough to know that long- and short-term objectives are being specified in individualized educational plans (IEPs) and that the documents are being reviewed in accordance with federal mandates. School personnel now want to know if students are learning at rates commensurate with their ability and handicap. They want to know if their assessment procedures place students in the most appropriate programs and if these procedures provide useful information to guide instruction. They want to judge the effects of individual programs and identify areas where improvements must be made.

Within this context, program evaluation becomes an essential tool for school personnel. Through the use of such procedures, educators can document program needs, show how effective programs are in meeting intended goals, and identify specific elements in programs that can be improved. They can also rely on program evaluation data to suggest ways in which they might go about making program improvements.

Why Evaluate?

Unfortunately, despite the growing need for program evaluation in special education, efforts to conduct such evaluations often have been planned and conducted only in response to external requests or legal mandates rather than being initiated internally by school personnel to serve their own unique purposes. Perhaps this is true, in part, because school personnel feel they lack the knowledge and the skills necessary to conduct a sound program evaluation (a problem this guide is designed to address). Or it may be because they feel they are already participating in sufficient program evaluation activities as part of their mandated compliance-monitoring efforts. They might feel that adding internally driven evaluation to their existing range of activities simply would prove to be too much. It may also be that school personnel do not fully realize the range of ways in which program evaluation can be used to serve their direct needs, or that evaluation doesn't necessarily have to involve cumbersome, time-consuming activities. In short, school personnel may not have a clear understanding of the good that can come from program evaluation and how they can gain those benefits without adding impossible burdens to their already demanding schedules.

There are many pragmatic reasons for school personnel to initiate and conduct evaluations of special programs and of the issues and problems related to these programs. For example, evaluation can provide useful information to document needs and support requests for additional resources. It may be that the instructional resources and assessment materials available at a particular school are inadequate to meet the needs of students with a particular type of handicap. Or perhaps a particular school has a need for more special education faculty. In each instance, requests for more resources are more likely to be granted if they are accompanied by evaluative evidence.

Consider, for example, the following case: The special education teachers at a large middle school were being asked constantly to assist regular class teachers in making accommodations for special students in their classes. Unfortunately, although they agreed that this was important, the special education teachers' schedules would not permit them to accommodate these requests routinely. Rather than continuing to lament this problem, the special educators devised a simple way of keeping track of mainstream teachers' requests for assistance, as well as a system for counting how often and to what extent they were able to respond to these requests. They also developed a system for monitoring the class grades of students with whose teachers they consulted. As a result of conducting these self-initiated evaluation activities over the course of two grading periods, the special education teachers had sufficient evidence to support a request that an additional "consulting" teacher be added to the staff. Their data showed that they had many more requests for assistance than were being handled and that students whose teachers made accommodations were performing better than those whose teachers were not.

In addition to providing information that can be used to support requests for resources, self-initiated program evaluation can also provide specific information about program strengths and weaknesses that can be used to make special education programs better. Are there particular aspects of the program that need to be improved or expanded? If so, what are they? Should certain aspects of the program be dropped completely or redesigned? You might want to know, for instance, whether the program provided for mildly handicapped students in your secondary school is placing sufficient emphasis on helping students develop the academic and social skills necessary for employment. In short, are they learning the kinds of things that will help them get a job and keep it, and if not, what kinds of things are being overlooked? These questions could be answered readily by collecting information directly from the students themselves, their parents, and/or their employers. Changes in the program could then be made accordingly as indicated by the responses obtained. Or it may be that responses indicate that no changes are warranted because the program is doing a good job of meeting your goal. In either event, information obtained through the evaluation activity would allow you to make the most effective decision.

What Program Evaluation Can Provide

Program evaluation can also provide a basis of comparison from which to judge the relative merits of instructional programs offered in special education classrooms. Imagine, for example, that you want to implement a new procedure for teaching spelling words to your resource-room students, a procedure that you discovered at a recent workshop. The procedure emphasizes guided use of a word-study technique, a distributed practice routine, and daily testing. This is quite a departure from your present system of teaching spelling, which involves a fair amount of student-directed activity. In order to use the new approach, you will have to make substantial changes in your classroom management plan, and you are wondering if it will be worth your effort to do so. By simply trying out the procedure on a limited basis (e.g., with two or three of your classes) and systematically collecting data on its effects, you will have the information you need to answer your questions. Did the students perform better as a result of the new procedure than they did under the old system? Was the extent of their improvement sufficient to make it worth your effort to change your classroom management plan? It may be that the data will show the new procedure is not significantly better than your old plan, and therefore its benefits might not outweigh the problems you would have to address in order to implement it.

Self-initiated program evaluation activities can also be extremely useful in helping prepare for, or respond to, external reviews of special education programs. For instance, school personnel might decide to prepare for mandatory evaluation by the state department of education by conducting their own study of program quality well in advance of their scheduled visit by state officials. This evaluation might focus on the same areas of concern or standards of quality that will be of interest to the external reviewers. In this instance, school personnel would be using program evaluation procedures diagnostically; that is, they would be attempting to identify for themselves aspects of their special education program that must be improved in order to pass the subsequent external review. This same "diagnostic" approach can also be employed after the fact in instances where programs have been reviewed externally and found to be nonstandard with respect to certain criteria. With this information in hand, school personnel could implement their own program evaluations designed to tell them specifically where changes should be made and what the nature of those changes should be.

This guide to the evaluation of special education programs reflects a belief that school personnel can do much to improve the quality of the instructional programs and service-delivery options in their schools by systematically evaluating program quality using criteria found to be associated with effective special education programs. By routinely engaging in evaluation activities, school personnel can make informed decisions about all aspects of programming, whether they involve broad questions of special education practice that can only be answered through extensive evaluation or smaller concerns that confront special educators daily and can be addressed in very simple ways. In either case, program evaluations can provide important information to document needs, support program changes, and identify promising alternatives.

The Purpose of This Guide

This guide was written with an eye toward encouraging school personnel to think of evaluation as being more than an externally mandated activity to which they must respond. It attempts to show that self-initiated evaluations can be valuable tools for meeting teachers' and principals' own purposes and doing so on their own terms. It also reflects an assumption that special educators can develop the knowledge and skills necessary to conduct useful evaluations. Within this context, this guide is intended to assist special educators in the study of the effectiveness and quality of their special education programs by providing tools to aid in planning and conducting evaluations within classrooms, in schools, or across a school system.

This guide was written for all educators concerned with special education programming within their schools. Because it gives direction to setting priorities among the needs of special education programs, it is expected that special education directors, coordinators, and teachers will use it with greatest frequency. The guide may also be beneficial, however, for those who work in related areas. For example, a school counselor who is working with high school juniors in preparing them for transition into postsecondary institutions may be interested in how the special education program prepares mildly handicapped students for such a transition.

Introduction 5

Who This Guide Is Intended to Serve

A wide range of instructional programs and service-delivery options are covered by this guide. It contains a set of standards and indicators of quality that cut across grade levels, disability categories, and service-delivery models. These standards and indicators are directly applicable to any type of special education program in elementary, middle-grade, or high school settings and can also be used to evaluate aspects of special education programs for preschool-age children with special needs. A second set of standards and indicators unique to secondary-level special education programs is also included, as is a third set dealing specifically with programs for the severely and profoundly handicapped. The additional standards and indicators can be used to guide evaluations in these specific program areas. The scope of all the standards and indicators includes academic, vocational, and self-help concerns and can therefore be used to evaluate a range of curricular alternatives.

This guide was written to be used by practitioners, not professional evaluators, and is not intended to serve as a comprehensive text on program evaluation. We have attempted to make it "user friendly" by using many concrete examples, by using nontechnical language, and by presenting examples of practical and feasible evaluation designs that can be adapted readily by school professionals to evaluate aspects of their special education programs. It is expected, however, that this guide will be used in conjunction with the initial volume in this series, *Evaluating School Programs: An Educator's Guide,* which provides an important introduction to the evaluation of school programs by school personnel.

What Is in the Guide

The first step in preparing this guide was to review and synthesize a great deal of literature on the characteristics of effective special education programs for the purpose of developing the list of standards and indicators of program quality described above (see Resource A). This list was developed with several assumptions in mind.

First, it was assumed that program evaluation data would be collected primarily at the school level by school personnel and that persons involved in the evaluation activities would be doing so in addition to carrying out their routine responsibilities. As a result, standards and indicators that could not be measured precisely and adequately without excessive time commitments were not included. Indicators of quality suggested in the literature that lacked sufficient empirical support were also excluded. Finally, it was decided to include a number of standards that are similar to legal compliance standards. These were judged to be among the most critical for effective special education programming; it was felt they should be evaluated in ways that illustrate varying degrees of quality (i.e., increments of effectiveness) beyond minimal compliance.

The list of standards and indicators presented in Resource A is an essential part of this guide, because it can be used to help focus evaluation of special education programs. Reviewing the list will help you identify aspects of your program that might be evaluated and define which qualities and characteristics of the program you will examine.

The body of the guide contains a series of vignettes that will take you through the major tasks of preparing for and conducting an evaluation of special education programs. This section is linked closely to the general guide (*Evaluating School Programs: An Educator's Guide*) in that it shows in great detail how procedures described in the latter could be applied to the evaluation of special education programs. The reader is shown in the general guide that planning, designing, and conducting an evaluation involves an orderly sequence of steps that includes such activities as (a) specifying the purposes of the evaluation, (b) determining who will receive the results, (c) focusing the evaluation, (d) determining who will conduct and manage the evaluation, (e) determining the resources available for the evaluation, (f) determining a time frame for the evaluation, (g) selecting methods for collecting and analyzing evaluation data, and (h) interpreting the results of the evaluation. Through the vignettes presented in this guide, you will learn what these steps might actually look like in practice when applied to special education concerns.

Each vignette provides a comprehensive example to serve as a guide for school personnel who may wish to carry out similar activities in their own settings. In each case, the vignette begins with a brief scenario outlining a rationale for conducting the evaluation activities that follow. This section is intended to show the reader what school personnel hope to accomplish through the evaluation, what their motivation is, and what question(s) they hope to answer. It also identifies specific standards and indicators of quality that will be the foci of the evaluation; these have been drawn from the list of standards and indicators presented in Resource A. The reader is directed to the second chapter of *Evaluating School Programs: An Educator's Guide* for a more detailed discussion of additional sources that might be used to focus an evaluation.

Following the description of the evaluation context, the reader is introduced to a data collection strategy that is appropriate to the question of interest. This section includes discussion of various data sources and approaches to data collection that might be considered. One data collection strategy is then illustrated in detail, including presentation of sample data collection instruments. The vignette concludes with a detailed description of how the data collected might be summarized, interpreted, and applied.

Each vignette is followed by a summary of important evaluation principles that were followed throughout the example. Also included is an overview of alternatives to the strategy used, including a sum-

Introduction

mary of pros and cons associated with each, and a discussion of cautions regarding the ways in which results could be misinterpreted.

The vignettes were selected because they addressed questions felt to be among those most commonly asked by special educators interested in evaluating their programs. Thus the examples can serve as a point of departure for those who may want to explore these same questions in their own setting. Perhaps more important, the vignettes are intended to provide insight into the evaluation process by showing in detail how one might implement the strategies and principles described in the general guide when evaluating specific special education strategies and approaches. The vignettes show the reader how special educators work together and with other school personnel in doing real evaluations of special education programs. Knowledge of this process will allow the reader to go well beyond the illustrations presented in this guide to evaluate their own school's special education programs effectively.

In order to get the most from this guide, it is recommended that you begin by carrying out the following steps. First, you should review *Evaluating School Programs: An Educator's Guide* for a comprehensive overview of the major issues that must be addressed in planning and implementing a program evaluation. This is ultimately where you will turn to get additional information on how to carry out the types of evaluations illustrated here. Next, you should skim this guide to get an idea of what it contains, especially with respect to the range of evaluation activities illustrated in the vignettes. Finally, you should review the set of standards and indicators of quality presented in Resource A to gain a sense of the dimensions of special education programs on which an evaluation might focus.

How to Use This Guide

Once this preliminary review of materials has been completed, you will be ready to use the guides to carry out the steps of planning, designing, and conducting a special education program evaluation. As a first step in this process, you will need to determine which parts of the special education program will be evaluated.

The focus for your evaluation can stem from a myriad of questions or concerns that you or someone else may have about the current special education program in your school or district, such as those illustrated in this guide's scenarios. Whatever your reason for beginning to look at an element of your special education program, it is important to identify the particular purpose or specific question(s) to be addressed in an evaluation. An evaluation must be planned carefully for the results to be of real value. One useful way to do this would be to meet as a group with those who are interested in conducting an evaluation. The listing of standards and indicators presented in Resource A can be used to provide ideas and materials to stimulate discussion and help focus the evaluation. Discussion should also center on the following questions, as well as those presented in the second chapter of the general guide:

1. Why is the program being evaluated? Is it being done for your own purposes, or are you responding to an external request? What led to the decision to evaluate?
2. Who will use the results, and how will they be used? What decisions or actions might occur based on the results?
3. Which issues surrounding your program will be evaluated? What are the most pressing concerns? Which program components are most relevant to the decisions and actions that might occur as a result of the evaluation? Which are the most critical for your purposes?
4. What resources are available to plan and complete the evaluation? Who will be involved? How much time will it take? Are funds available for materials and supplies?

By addressing each of these points, the group can conceptualize the type of evaluation to be conducted and determine what the results should produce. This information, in turn, will assist you in preparing appropriate data collection strategies and also in choosing the staff who will be involved. To get a better idea of how the process of focusing an evaluation might evolve in practice, review the section entitled "Focusing the Evaluation" in each of the vignettes that follow.

What Should I Evaluate?

Once the purpose and general focus for your evaluation have been established, the group needs to develop a specific plan for conducting the evaluation. This plan must address issues related to the who, what, where, and when of the evaluation. In short, in developing the plan, consideration should be given to the full range of details that will be involved in carrying out the evaluation. Typically, the types of questions the group will need to address include the following:

- Who will lead the evaluation project, and who will work on it?
- What sources of information will be used, and how will the information be collected? What resources will be needed to get the information? What financial constraints must be addressed?
- If instruments (e.g., surveys, questionnaires, checklists) are to be used, who will locate or develop them? Will data collectors need to be trained?
- How will participants be selected, and what will be done to maintain confidentiality? Is informed consent needed? How will it be obtained?
- How will data be tabulated and analyzed once they are obtained, and who will be responsible for doing it?
- What criteria will be used to judge the outcomes? What procedures will be used to make those judgments?

Introduction 9

- What time line will be used to prepare for and implement the project? Are there important deadlines that must be considered?
- What reports of outcomes or other products will be made, and who will receive them? Who will prepare these materials?

How Will I Do the Evaluation?

Answers to these questions will provide a framework for developing a comprehensive plan to guide the evaluation. The importance of addressing these concerns at the outset cannot be overemphasized. Without a clearly thought-out plan, evaluators run the risk of investing substantial time and energy conducting evaluations that may not provide them with relevant or valid information. In contrast, well-planned and carefully organized evaluations typically provide important information that can guide sound planning and decision making.

As you begin to map out the specifics of your evaluation plan, you should review chapters 2 and 3 of *Evaluating School Programs: An Educator's Guide,* which provide detailed information to assist you. These chapters discuss approaches for narrowing the focus of your evaluation and specifying evaluation questions to guide your efforts. Also included is information on common data sources, and methods for collecting data. You will find the planning worksheets provided in figures 2.1 and 2.2 of the general guide to be especially useful at this point in helping you develop a sound evaluation plan.

The vignettes contained in this guide can also be quite useful in showing you how to plan your evaluation. Each of them has a section entitled "How to Evaluate" that will give you a feel for how the evaluation-planning process evolves. Moreover, the vignettes can be used as a reference tool to show you how various strategies for collecting evaluative information might be implemented. They were specifically organized to illustrate a range of data collection approaches commonly used in program evaluation, including use of: questionnaires, surveys, needs assessments, direct observation, checklists, document reviews, and standardized instruments. Once your evaluation has been focused and evaluation questions have been identified, the vignettes can serve as models for how you might address your questions.

In addition to using the vignettes in this guide to assist you in planning an evaluation, you can also take advantage of several other features of the guide. Each of the standards and indicators of quality provided in Resource A includes a listing of suggested data collection strategies that might be used in evaluating that standard or indicator. The standards and indicators also have been referenced to the vignettes that illustrate use of particular strategies. Thus, when you review Resource A as part of your early efforts to focus your evaluation, you will also get a sense of how you might assess various dimensions of your program and which vignettes apply most directly. Finally, a list of references designed to assist you in several ways is given in Resource B. The list provides examples of sources you can consult to obtain additional information about the evaluation strategies illustrated in the vignettes and described in the general guide. It also includes sources that illustrate alternative evaluation strategies; these can be used when the evaluation strategy associated with selected standards and indicators does not appear in any vignette included in this guide. The references also include additional summaries of quality standards for special education programs and examples of special education evaluation studies that utilize strategies similar to those shown in the vignettes.

1 Vignette One

Teacher Needs for Staff Development

Where, What, and Why

Lawsonville School is located in Clinton, a rural town of 5,000 people. Surrounded by several large family farms, with tobacco, cotton, peaches, and pecans as major crops, Clinton is rapidly growing into a less rural, more suburban small town. Changes over the years in the economic feasibility of farming (tobacco farming in particular) as a means of livelihood have given rise to the development of small industry in the area, especially textiles and small appliances. Once a K-8 school for the children of farmers in the surrounding countryside, Lawsonville School now enrolls children whose cultural and socioeconomic backgrounds are quite diverse. In addition to the children of local landowners, tenant farmers, and migrant workers, the school now serves families who have moved to the area to work in the factories, in management as well as on the assembly line. In recent years, Clinton has become a desirable place to live, attracting an increasing number of wealthy families who chose to leave the big city and enjoy a slower-paced rural setting for raising their families.

Teachers at Lawsonville have been challenged in recent years to provide appropriate educational experiences for an increasingly diverse student population. Free exchange of ideas has been a strength at Lawsonville, largely because of the efforts of Mr. Robert Watts, a veteran teacher and now principal of Lawsonville for the fifth year. As he listens to the comments of faculty members during faculty meetings and during casual conversations, he notes the following: Mrs. Denise Holmes, a school counselor, says that she is getting larger and larger numbers of referrals of students with behavior problems. Mrs. Talbert, a fifth-grade teacher, is one of several classroom teachers who have expressed interest in finding out more about learning disabilities, noticing that some of their children seem to need more help than they feel prepared to give in the classroom. Dena Kennedy, a first-year teacher, has indicated an interest in attention deficit-hyperactivity disorder (ADHD), a topic she studied in college; she wonders if some of the "behavior problems" might not be examined more appropriately in terms of attention problems. Mrs. Yelton, the resource teacher, expresses her opinion that all students, not just those with special needs, would benefit from more individualized instruction in their classrooms. It is readily apparent to Mr. Watts that his faculty would likely enjoy and benefit from staff development activities related to some of these problems; he gives this item top priority as he prepares the agenda for the next faculty meeting.

Ideas for In-Service Workshops

As the Lawsonville faculty began to consider ideas for in-service workshops, they were very appreciative of the fact that their judgments had been invited. Lively discussion ensued, and it became apparent that the possible range of topics was quite wide. Mr. Watts wisely suggested that a small committee be formed to narrow the field. He also noted that many of the ideas discussed related to "special needs" students, and, therefore, he asked Mrs. Yelton to chair the committee. Ms. Holmes and Mrs. Talbert volunteered for this committee and Mr. Watts appointed Ms. Kennedy, believing that she had much to contribute but was probably reluctant to volunteer because of her limited experience in the classroom. The committee planned to meet the following day after school; members were asked to come with a list of what they believed were the most pressing in-service training needs for Lawsonville's faculty, especially with regard to special education students.

Focus for the Evaluation

Mr. Watts attended the committee's first meeting and shared the newly published Essential Tools for Educators (ETE) series. He referred them to the general guide (*Evaluating School Programs: An Educator's Guide*) and to *Special Education Programs: A Guide to Evaluation* and directed their attention to Resource A in the latter, which delineates a set of standards and indicators to guide evaluation efforts. He pointed out Standard 2, which states, "Quality special education programs involve all personnel who work with handicapped students in appropriate training to strengthen their ability to provide effective services." Mrs. Yelton noted that Indicator 2.2 seemed particularly relevant; it reads, "Topics offered for in-service training sessions are identified on the basis of the school's specific program needs." The committee members agreed that this indicator would be the focus of their evaluation efforts. Mr. Watts left them with a copy of each guide to use as reference tools.

How to Evaluate?

As the committee looked at their individually prepared lists of needs for in-service training, they began to recognize the magnitude of concerns surrounding the needs of exceptional individuals in the classroom. They concluded that, although their collective list seemed long enough, they would be well-advised to take a look at some current professional literature to identify any additional areas they might have overlooked. Ms. Kennedy and Mrs. Yelton both offered to bring some professional journals, and Mrs. Holmes, who commutes from Asheville (which houses a state university campus), volunteered to visit the university library for other sources. The teachers identified several articles related to their efforts and found that they were able to combine elements from each with their own list, resulting in an extensive list of possible topics for in-service training at Lawsonville School.

First Draft of Questionnaire

Mrs. Yelton, who has a master's degree in special education, recalled a course on evaluation of educational programs that she had found particularly helpful. Aware of the importance of expert guidance, she reviewed her notes from the course and decided to share them with the committee at their next meeting. She suggested to the group that perhaps their next step might be to survey the faculty to get an indication of which topics the faculty and staff might find most useful. Referring to Chapter 3 of the general guide, the committee reviewed various survey possibilities (e.g., written questionnaire, telephone questionnaire, interview) and surmised that in their situation, a written questionnaire might be the most expedient method of securing the information they wanted. They consulted Resource B of the special education program evaluation guide for references to guide their development of the survey instrument. Mrs. Yelton and Mrs. Holmes worked together on the first draft of the questionnaire, and then the committee met to edit it as necessary. As revisions were being made, they were careful to review the general guide to make sure they had not violated any principles of sound program evaluation. Aware of the need to encourage prompt response, they made efforts to keep the questionnaire as simple as possible.

Measurement Instrument

As the committee took a final look at their list of training needs, they noticed that many of the items related to assessment of learner characteristics and needs; they also noticed that several items related to instructional concerns. Mrs. Holmes suggested that they might keep these categories in mind when they begin to summarize and interpret the data they obtain. Having completed the lists of possible topics for consideration for staff development, Mrs. Yelton's committee designed its questionnaire so that each area of interest was evaluated in two ways: (a) the extent to which the respondent feels training in an area would be useful, and (b) the extent to which the respondent feels a topic has already been addressed in earlier training. Consulting the general guide once more, the committee selected the format that seemed best suited for collecting the data they needed. Their final version is represented in Figure 1.1.

Results

The questionnaires were distributed at the conclusion of the next full faculty meeting with instructions to place the completed questionnaires in Mr. Watts's box by 3:00 the following afternoon. Mr. Watts explained the purpose and goals of the evaluation to his staff and encouraged their participation. He told them that they need not use their names in completing the questionnaire, because he was interested primarily in assessing needs for the school as a whole. Of the total group of 28 possible respondents (16 classroom teachers, 4 specialists, and 8 assistants), 23 responded the next day. Committed to his desire for 100% participation, Mr. Watts sent a memo to the faculty urging those who had not yet responded to do so, reminding them that the results would be used to plan a staff development agenda designed to address their stated needs. Following this reminder, the remaining 5 questionnaires were returned, thus establishing a 100% response rate.

Summarization of Data

Mrs. Yelton and Mrs. Holmes worked together to summarize the data so that they could interpret the teachers' responses to the needs assessment survey. They counted the number of teachers who selected each response category for each of the 31 training areas. To make the results easier to understand, they then converted the number of responses in each response category to a percentage. Mrs. Yelton

Grade Level: _____

For each of the items in this survey, we are interested in (a) the extent to which you feel a workshop of this nature would be useful to you, and (b) the extent to which you feel this topic has already been satisfactorily addressed in previous in-service training. Please indicate two responses for each item using the following keys:

Left-Hand Column
1. Extremely useful
2. Quite useful
3. Somewhat useful
4. Of minimal use
5. Not at all useful

Right-Hand Column
1. Thoroughly addressed, no additional training needed
2. Well addressed, minimal additional training needed
3. Competently covered, but additional training needed
4. Minimally covered, substantial additional training needed
5. Not addressed at all, substantial additional training needed

Useful / *Addressed*

1. Behavioral and learning characteristics of learning disabled students
2. Behavioral and learning characteristics of students with attention deficit disorder
3. Behavioral and learning characteristics of mentally handicapped students
4. Recent research on teaching exceptional children in the least restrictive environment and the rationale for mainstreaming
5. Various mainstreaming models (e.g., consulting teacher, itinerant teacher, resource room, self-contained classroom)
6. State and federal legislation concerning education of exceptional children
7. Legal rights of parents and students under Public Law 94-142 and other special education laws
8. Teacher rights, liabilities, and ethical responsibilities under special education
9. Identifying a student's learning style characteristics or behavior patterns
10. Gathering information to determine students' individual needs
11. Identifying students in need of special education services
12. Identifying and implementing appropriate individualized intervention strategies
13. Interpreting and utilizing psychoeducational test data, reports, and recommendations
14. Identifying ways to assess and/or evaluate academic achievement or progress of exceptional students
15. Developing fair and appropriate tests and grading systems for exceptional students
16. Establishing a classroom climate and designing teaching procedures that accept and provide for individual differences
17. Applying the results of diagnostic tests, classroom observations, and parent information in developing individual goals that are appropriate, realistic, and measurable
18. Classroom organization and management techniques (e.g., record-keeping, time management and planning) that facilitate individualization in mainstream classrooms
19. Developing a variety of alternative teaching strategies to accomplish each goal
20. Developing learning centers to facilitate instruction
21. Utilizing the assistance of volunteers (e.g., peer tutors, older students, parents) to reinforce classroom instruction
22. Developing lesson plans that meet the instructional needs of both regular and exceptional students in the classroom

____ 23. Locating and using materials and methods that help students compensate ____
for disabilities (e.g., tape recorder, visual aids, large-print books)
____ 24. Methods of modifying teaching to vary presentation, practice, and testing ____
requirements based on student learning-style characteristics and level of functioning
____ 25. Teaching study skills and learning strategies within the context of instruction ____
____ 26. The use of cognitive and metacognitive strategies with exceptional students in the ____
mainstream classroom
____ 27. The use of technology (e.g., computer hardware and software, audiovisual ____
equipment) to enhance learning
____ 28. Applying behavior management principles or techniques with exceptional students ____
____ 29. Motivation theory and techniques ____
____ 30. Reinforcement theory and techniques ____
____ 31. Communicating effectively with parents of exceptional students ____

Please use the following space to indicate any other areas of concern to you in your efforts to meet the needs of exceptional students in your classroom. In particular, list topics for which you would like an in-service workshop.

Figure 1.1. Needs Assessment Survey for Lawsonville School

summarized the results for the left-hand column of the questionnaire, while Mrs. Holmes summarized the responses to the questions on the right. The results are shown in Table 1.1.

Interpretation

The results clearly indicated a strong interest on the part of most Lawsonville faculty and staff members in staff development activities related to the instructional needs of exceptional students in the mainstream classroom. High percentages of teachers responded "extremely useful" to those items addressing the modification of teaching techniques or classroom environments in order to improve instruction for exceptional students. A fairly high level of interest also was noted in response to items concerned with student assessment. In contrast, items dealing with theory, research, and public laws received fairly low percentages of teacher interest. One notable exception within this broad category was the eighth item, relating to teacher liabilities, for which 96% of the respondents indicated "extremely useful" or "quite useful."

Use of Results

The results and their interpretation served to confirm Mr. Watts's initial belief that many of Lawsonville School's specific program needs

TABLE 1.1 Summary of Needs Assessment Survey

	Percentage of Responses by Category									
	Useful					Addressed				
	1	2	3	4	5	1	2	3	4	5
Assessment Concerns										
1. LD characteristics and needs	71	22	7	0	0	0	0	7	86	7
2. ADHD characteristics and needs	64	29	7	0	0	0	0	4	82	14
3. EMH characteristics and needs	71	22	7	0	0	0	4	4	86	6
9. Learning style	25	36	36	3	0	0	4	36	32	32
10. Individual needs	79	18	3	0	0	0	0	4	89	7
11. Identifying students	68	18	11	3	0	0	14	18	61	7
13. Interpreting data	75	18	7	0	0	0	4	7	85	4
14. Evaluating progress	64	25	11	0	0	0	4	17	75	4
15. Developing fair tests	68	21	11	0	0	0	0	14	72	14
Instructional Concerns										
5. Models	73	23	36	2	5	4	4	14	53	25
12. Intervention strategies	86	14	0	0	0	0	4	7	79	10
16. Classroom climate	64	25	11	0	0	4	7	14	72	4
17. Developing goals	75	21	4	0	0	4	4	10	75	7
18. Classroom organization and management	89	11	0	0	0	7	14	54	14	11
19. Alternative strategies	86	14	0	0	0	0	0	7	86	7
20. Learning centers	71	18	11	0	0	0	4	14	71	11
21. Volunteer tutors	68	18	14	0	0	0	3	11	11	75
22. Instructional planning	86	11	3	0	0	0	0	7	68	25
23. Materials	89	7	4	0	0	0	0	14	75	11
24. Modification of teaching methods	75	18	7	0	0	0	0	11	11	78
25. Study skills	64	18	18	0	0	0	0	0	14	86
26. Cognitive and metacognitive strategies	68	21	11	0	0	0	0	0	3	97
27. Computer and technology	86	14	0	0	0	0	0	4	7	89
Other Concerns										
4. Research/Mainstreaming	7	25	50	14	4	4	11	54	14	17
6. Legislation	7	25	46	18	4	4	11	50	21	14
7. Legal rights of parents	7	29	50	14	0	0	0	4	21	75
8. Teacher liabilities	89	7	4	0	0	0	0	4	7	89
28. Behavior management	71	18	11	0	0	4	4	25	60	7
29. Motivation theory	14	36	50	0	0	4	7	14	71	4
30. Reinforcement theory	11	32	54	3	0	4	4	75	3	4
31. Communication with parents	79	14	7	0	0	4	10	18	61	7

were related to appropriate training for all faculty and staff who work with exceptional children. Because of increased efforts to mainstream children, training should necessarily involve all teachers and assistants.

Using the percentages of teacher responses, Mrs. Yelton's committee developed a list of potential in-service training topics in order of priority. Given the extent of interest and the number of areas to be addressed, they decided to propose a workshop series that would consist of six 2-hour sessions, with meetings every other Tuesday. Each session would be designed to address one or more of the priority topics identified from the survey. Alternate Tuesdays were reserved for regular faculty meetings over the course of the next 3 months. Working with the director of programs for exceptional children from the school system's administrative offices, Mrs. Yelton and Mr. Watts presented the following proposed workshop schedule to the committee for approval. It subsequently was endorsed by the faculty and scheduled to begin the next week.

> *Workshop Title:* Meeting the Needs of the Exceptional Child in the Regular Classroom
>
> *Session 1:* Teacher Liabilities and Public Law
>
> *Session 2:* Classroom Organization and Management
>
> *Session 3:* Instructional Assessment Planning
>
> *Session 4:* Materials and Technology
>
> *Session 5:* Strategies for Intervention: Alternative Teaching Techniques
>
> *Session 6:* Teaching Learning Strategies to Exceptional Students (Study Skills, Cognitive and Metacognitive Strategies)

Summary of Evaluation Principles

Several important principles should be kept in mind in all evaluations of school programs. As in other examples in this guide, a list of these principles is provided here:

1. Do not attempt to evaluate every aspect of a program at once. Focus the evaluation by selecting a few indicators of quality from the list in Resource A.
2. When choosing a method of data collection, try to select one that minimizes the burden on those who will be asked to provide information and can be implemented well given your resources and timetable.
3. Whenever appropriate, inform participants about the evaluation goals and allow voluntary participation. Guarantee confidentiality; if appropriate, provide anonymity.
4. When the group of interest is small, collecting information from everyone is better than collecting information from a sample. Conclusions should be based on "all teachers" or "all students in grade 8" whenever possible.
5. Collect information that will help to identify program strengths and weaknesses, and guide action when improvement is needed. The

data you gather should be as specific as possible. Vague or general information will tell you little about your program.
6. Whenever possible, seek redundant information. Ask several questions about each important evaluation topic.

Alternatives to the Questionnaire Strategy

Because Indicator 2.2 stated that in-service training sessions are to be identified on the basis of specific program needs, faculty and staff were the obvious source of information. This information might also have been gained through group meetings, individual interviews, or open-ended questionnaires. The written questionnaire method was selected in this case for a variety of reasons. The benefit of group discussion in raising consciousness levels was accomplished during the first full faculty meetings; beyond that, the large group might have proved too cumbersome to be effective in arriving at group consensus. Individual interviews represent an alternative method of data collection that offers the benefit of personal contact, but they can be costly in terms of personnel time. Open-ended questionnaires, although conducive to free expression of opinion, might not lead easily to identification of priority training needs. The survey as designed combined the benefits of insights gained from open-ended questions with those of a well-constructed list of items that were specific in their description of desired competencies. Evaluators are reminded that every organization has its own unique set of characteristics and needs. Choices among alternative data collection methods should be approached with deliberate attention to these unique needs. (See Chapter 3 of *Evaluating School Programs: An Educator's Guide* for more detailed discussion of alternative methods of data collection.)

Possible Misinterpretations

One possible misinterpretation of these results would be that classroom teachers' and assistants' priorities are the only indicators of specific program needs. Although they are certainly knowledgeable about their own requirements on a day-to-day basis, it is likely that, similar to practitioners, teachers and assistants tend to relegate theory and matters of law to a disproportionately low position in their own hierarchies. In fact, these areas are very much part of the overall effectiveness of instructional programs. The wise administrator or staff development planner will find ways to mesh theory with practice and will weave the essentials of public school law, as related to exceptional children, into a workshop plan. The administrator or planner should also seek the advice of specialists outside the school before finalizing a workshop schedule.

2

Vignette Two

Appropriateness of Least Restrictive Environment (LRE) Placements

Where, What, and Why

Scottsdale School District is located 10 miles southwest of a midsize metropolitan area in rural Virginia. The local community is supported by a variety of agricultural industries. There is also a midsize college located nearby that employs many of the residents of this community. Many of the residents of the Scottsdale District are professors or students from the local college. The Scottsdale students' families are racially as well as socioeconomically diverse. About 35% of the school's pupils are black; the rest are white.

Scottsdale School is a large elementary school serving grades K-5, with a total of three classrooms per grade. There are two resource rooms that serve a large population of students who have been identified as mildly handicapped. At the beginning of this year a new principal, Dr. Cohen, who just received her Ph.D. in special education (with a minor in educational administration) from the nearby college, was appointed to the school. Dr. Cohen, because of her background in special education, was very interested in the mainstreaming movement. She knew the least restrictive environment (LRE) mandates of P.L. 94-142 had necessitated close working relationships between regular and special educators. During the in-service meetings held before the school year began, Dr. Cohen asked the special education teachers to discuss their concerns about the school's past mainstreaming efforts.

Both special education teachers raised their concern that too many mildly handicapped students were being referred for services. They felt that many of the learning disabled (LD) students who were mainstreamed during the past year had a great deal of difficulty managing the requirements of their mainstream classes. One resource teacher, Ms. Rice, felt strongly that many of these students' academic and behavior problems were a function of factors in the mainstream instructional environment. The other resource teacher, Mr. Moss, felt that referral could have been avoided for many students had the special education teachers been better able to provide instructional assistance to the regular teachers. Ms. Rice suggested that if they had a clearer picture of the mainstream instructional environment, they could prepare their special students better and also assist teachers in designing appropriate instructional interventions within the regular class environment for these children.

Problems of Mainstreaming

Dr. Cohen suggested that an evaluation committee be formed to help resolve the problems of mainstreaming. Because the issues discussed related directly to the mildly handicapped student population, she appointed Ms. Rice to chair the committee. Mr. Moss and two regular classroom teachers—Ms. Green and Mrs. Sobel—volunteered because of their concern that many mildly handicapped students had difficulty in the mainstream classes. The committee decided it would be useful for them to seek out some "expert guidance" from within the district to assist them in their evaluation efforts, because no one in the group felt they had sufficient experience in conducting this type of evaluation. The special education supervisor for Scottsdale School, Mrs. Jones, agreed to serve in this capacity. The committee prepared to meet the following day after school. Members were asked to come to the meeting with a list of children who presently were mainstreamed into the regular classrooms.

Focus for the Evaluation

Dr. Cohen attended the first meeting of the evaluation team and shared a copy each of *Evaluating School Programs: An Educator's Guide* and *Special Education Programs: A Guide to Evaluation*. She directed everyone's attention to Standard 6 in Resource A, which read, "Quality programs for handicapped students' exceed minimal compliance standards with respect to maximizing students' participation in the regular education program with nonhandicapped peers." Dr. Cohen noted that Indicator 6.2 ("School personnel make every effort to serve exceptional students in the least restrictive setting possible") seemed particularly relevant, because the evaluation team was interested in determining the extent to which accommodation for special education students took place in the mainstreamed classes and not just how many handicapped students attended mainstream classes; moreover, they wanted to get a sense of how appropriate their accommodation efforts were. The committee members agreed that this indicator should guide their evaluation of the quality of their mainstreaming efforts in Scottsdale School. Dr. Cohen also suggested that committee members read the general guide to assist them in planning the evaluation.

How to Evaluate?

The committee members met and discussed many ways that they could obtain information about the quality of the mainstreaming efforts in their school. The first suggestion made was that teachers be asked to complete a questionnaire about their instructional environment and how they adjusted their classes to fit the needs of special students (see Chapter 3 in the general guide for discussion of questionnaires). Yet it was felt that results obtained through this approach could be somewhat biased, in that many teachers might report one thing while implementing something quite different in their classes. Another suggestion made was that students should be surveyed to discuss the difficulties they encountered in meeting the goals of the mainstream classes they attend. This strategy was also rejected, however, for several reasons. It was felt that the information collected in this manner might also be biased, or that many of the students might be unable to articulate their difficulties accurately. The committee members also rejected this idea because they felt it would not adequately assist them in diagnosing potential problem areas that cut across the school; the committee wanted an approach that would lead to suggestions for improvement.

TIES Instrument

As the lively discussion continued, the principal entered and mentioned that during her doctoral studies she had heard about a new instrument called *The Instructional Environment Scale* (TIES; see Ysseldyke & Christenson, 1987, in Resource B) that was commercially available for assessing mainstream environments. This instrument, she explained, would enable the evaluation team to describe the school's mainstream class instructional environments systematically and would result in an inventory of instructional strengths and needs critical to the design of effective instructional interventions for special students. Dr. Cohen emphasized that TIES is a standardized instrument only in the sense of providing a systematic approach to data collection. TIES does not provide normative data in the traditional sense, but it does allow one to look systematically at classroom environments. The committee decided to review TIES and to meet later in the week.

At the next meeting the committee was very excited because they had reached a consensus that the TIES instrument would allow them to take a random sample of mildly handicapped students who were mainstreamed and evaluate the quality of their mainstream instructional environments. Everyone agreed it would be too time consuming to observe all mainstreamed students and that such an approach was not necessary to obtain a reasonably accurate picture of the quality of mainstreaming efforts across the school. The committee decided initially to look at five mildly handicapped students' mainstream instructional environments. One class would be chosen for each elementary grade (kindergarten classes were omitted). The next time through this procedure, more students and their environments would be included.

The TIES instrument provided all the materials they would need, and the procedures seemed easy to follow. TIES is designed to gather data about the effectiveness of instructional environments as they relate to individual students. The committee, according to the directions in the TIES manual, would gather the data using three methods: interviewing the student's teacher, observing the student in a classroom setting, and interviewing the student directly. The data would then be used in an integrative manner to complete an instructional rating form that delineated 12 components found to be characteristics of effective classroom instruction. The committee believed that they could review the data from all five students to provide a general profile of the areas of mainstreaming strength and areas of needed improvement for the school as a whole.

Measurement Instrument

The committee prepared for the evaluation by completing a list of students who presently were mainstreamed; they then randomly chose one student in each grade level. The TIES instrument was reviewed by the resource teachers, who agreed to conduct the observations and the interviews. Dr. Cohen agreed that the observations and interviews would take some time, which was a rare commodity for her resource teachers. Mrs. Jones, the special education supervisor, agreed to serve as the resource instructor during the time that Ms. Rice and Mr. Moss would need to be away from their respective classes. Ms. Rice and Mr. Moss designed an observation and interview schedule in which Ms. Rice was responsible for the first and second grades and Mr. Moss would complete what would be needed for the third, fourth, and fifth grades. At most, the procedures they planned would take 1½ hours per class.

The TIES instrument provided easy-to-follow instructions on how to collect data on the 12 components of effective instruction. The 12 components are instructional presentation, classroom environment, teacher expectations, cognitive emphasis, motivational strategies, relevant practice, academic engaged time, informed feedback, adaptive instruction, progress evaluation, instructional planning, and student understanding. Figure 2.1 illustrates one student's profile in each of these components. Each of these components is described in detail in the TIES instrument so that users will know exactly what is meant by each term.

As Ms. Rice and Mr. Moss reviewed the TIES instrument, they noted its four parts: the data record form, the instructional rating form, the summary/profile sheet, and the descriptors. The first three of these items are shown in Figure 2.2.

Procedures

Successful Administration

Mr. Moss suggested to Ms. Rice that they set aside an afternoon to become familiar with the parts and the administration procedures of the instrument. They also sent a memo to all the teachers involved, letting them know what the process involved and why they would be conducting the observations and interviews. The next afternoon, the two of them read the description of each of the forms in the TIES instrument. Then, after becoming familiar with the detailed descriptions of each component, Ms. Rice and Mr. Moss agreed that successful administration of TIES would require completion of six steps per student in each grade. Ms. Rice, as mentioned, decided to seek information about the students in the first and second grades because she was often in the younger students' classes. Mr. Moss had offered to observe the third-, fourth- and fifth-grade classes. They determined that they would use the following sequence for administering the TIES instrument with each individual and his or her class:

1. Conduct a 30-minute classroom observation and complete the two middle pages of the data record form. As shown in Figure 2.2, this portion of the form contains 10 boxes in which to record observations related to 10 of the 12 instructional components assessed in TIES.
2. Interview the target student and complete the fourth page of the data record form shown in Figure 2.2. This page contains six brief questions concerning the mainstream environment that are directed to the student (e.g., "What does your teacher expect you to do when he or she gives these assignments?").
3. Interview the student's teacher and complete the first page of the data record form, also shown in Figure 2.2. This page contains seven

	Similarity to the Student's Instruction:			
	Not at All	Not Much	Somewhat	Very Much
1. Instructional presentation	1	②	3	4
2. Classroom environment	1	2	3	④
3. Teacher expectations	1	2	③	4
4. Cognitive emphasis	①	2	3	4
5. Motivational strategies	1	2	③	4
6. Relevant practice	1	2	③	4
7. Academic engaged time	1	2	③	4
8. Informed feedback	1	②	3	4
9. Adaptive instruction	1	2	3	④
10. Progress evaluation	1	2	3	④
11. Instructional planning	1	2	3	④
12. Student understanding	1	②	3	4

Figure 2.1. Sample Student Profile Using TIES Components

  questions directed to the teacher about the particular lesson that was observed.
4. Complete the instructional rating form and the summary profile sheet. The rating form lists the 12 components of effective instruction and allows judgments to be recorded for each component using a 4-point Likert scale.
5. Provide feedback to the teacher and student.
6. Prepare integrated summary forms and provide feedback to the committee.

Ms. Rice and Mr. Moss set up their observations of classroom instruction so that they would observe each teacher during basic skills instruction. The special education supervisor, Ms. Jones, had already agreed to take over Ms. Rice's and Mr. Moss's classes for the 1½ hour periods they would need to spend observing and interviewing. The observations were set to begin the following week and to continue for the next 5 weeks; this schedule was set because Mrs. Jones normally spent 1 day a week at this school. The resource teachers and Mrs. Jones

Text continued on p. 36

TIES
The Instructional Environment Scale

INSTRUCTIONAL RATING FORM

James E. Ysseldyke
Sandra L. Christenson

Student _____
Grade _____ Age _____
Examiner _____
Referred by _____ School _____
Dates of Observation _____
_____
Date of Teacher Interview _____
Date of Student Interview _____

Directions: Describe the instructional setting. Include length of the observation, instructional grouping arrangements, and number and kinds of tasks occurring.

Directions: Describe any atypical circumstances (e.g., fire alarms).

Copyright © 1987 by James E. Ysseldyke and Sandra L. Christenson

Additional copies of this form (#0647) may be purchased from PRO-ED, 5341 Industrial Oaks Blvd. Austin, Texas 78735 USA 512/892-3142

Figure 2.2. Sample Instructional Rating Form

Appropriateness of LRE Placements

INSTRUCTIONS

The TIES Instructional Rating Form contains statements about 12 components of effective instructional environments. Some statements describe the instructional environment of the student you are evaluating, others do not. After observation, teacher interview and student interview, rate the extent to which each statement characterizes the student's instructional environment. Select one of four possible ratings: 4 means the description is very much like the student's instructional environment; 3 means the description is somewhat like the student's instructional environment; 2 means the description is not much like the student's instructional environment; and 1 means the description is not at all like the student's instructional environment. Circle only one rating.

Very Much Like the Student's Instruction	Somewhat Like the Student's Instruction	Not Much Like the Student's Instruction	Not at All Like the Student's Instruction
4	3	2	1

---

1. **INSTRUCTIONAL PRESENTATION:** Instruction is presented in a clear and effective manner; directions contain sufficient information for the student to understand what kinds of behaviors or skills are to be demonstrated; and the student's understanding is checked before independent practice. This is to be evaluated by taking into account: 4 3 2 1

   Lesson Development
   - The student's attention is gained.
   - Prior skills or lessons are reviewed.
   - Instructional goals are specified and the student is told both why a task is important and told or shown how it may be accomplished.
   - Explanation is provided by demonstration, modeling, or use of several concrete examples.
   - Lesson presentation is organized in a step-by-step manner, and there is a high degree of teacher-student academic interaction about the skill to be learned.
   - The lesson moves at a pace that is appropriate to maintain the student's attention.

   Clarity of Directions
   - The student's attention is gained prior to delivery of oral directions.
   - Written or oral directions are given in easily understood language, are of appropriate length and number, and are given in the correct order.

   Checking for Student Understanding
   - Guided or controlled practice is used.
   - Teachers regularly check student understanding of what is being taught.
   - There is active monitoring of pupil performance during the first 5 or 10 minutes of seatwork practice activities.

2. **CLASSROOM ENVIRONMENT:** The classroom is controlled efficiently and effectively; there is a positive, supportive classroom atmosphere; time is used productively. This is to be evaluated by taking into account: 4 3 2 1

   Classroom Management
   - Classroom rules and procedures are clear.
   - Rules and procedures have been communicated clearly to the student during the first week of school.
   - Rules are reinforced consistently throughout the school year.
   - Behavioral disruptions are handled promptly.
   - The student knows the consequences of appropriate and inappropriate behavior.

   Productive Time Use
   - Transitions between activities are short.
   - There are few interruptions in the flow of classroom activities.
   - There is an academic, task-oriented focus in the classroom.
   - There is sufficient time allocated to academic activities.

   Class Climate
   - There is acceptance of individual differences.
   - Teacher-student interactions (for the target student) are positive.
   - For the target student, there is a supportive, cooperative atmosphere.

3. **TEACHER EXPECTATIONS:** There are realistic, yet high expectations for both the amount and accuracy of work to be completed, and these are communicated clearly to the student. This is to be evaluated by taking into account: 4 3 2 1
   - The student understands the teacher's expectations for the amount, neatness and accuracy of work to be completed.
   - The student understands how to demonstrate mastery of the instructional goal.
   - The student is held accountable for assigned work.
   - The student is expected to use classroom time productively.

4. **COGNITIVE EMPHASIS:** Thinking skills used in completing assignments are communicated explicitly to the student. This is to be evaluated by taking into account: 4 3 2 1
   - Thinking skills are clearly explained or modeled.
   - The teacher explains how and why the student's responses are correct and incorrect.
   - The student has had opportunity to explain the process used to complete the task.
   - Learning strategies are taught directly.

5. **MOTIVATIONAL STRATEGIES:** The teacher has and uses effective strategies for heightening student interest and effort. This is to be evaluated by taking into account: 4 3 2 1
   - The teacher shows enthusiasm for and interest in the material presented.
   - The student understands the importance of assigned tasks.
   - Instruction is designed to reflect the student's interests and experiences.
   - Extra motivational techniques (e.g., rewards, goal-setting) are used when appropriate.

6. **RELEVANT PRACTICE:** The student is given adequate opportunity to practice with appropriate materials. Classroom tasks are clearly important to achieving instructional goals. This is to be evaluated by taking into account: 4 3 2 1

   Practice Opportunity
   - The student achieves at least a 70% success rate on initial practice tasks.
   - The student is given ample time to engage in independent practice of skills at a 90-100% rate of success.
   - Drill and practice is continued until automaticity is achieved.

   Task Relevance
   - The instructional presentation, independent practice and assignments are related to the student's attainment of specific goals.

   Instructional Material
   - The student achieves an appropriate success rate on assigned tasks.
   - Skills are practiced in varied ways to facilitate generalization.
   - Different and supplemental materials (in addition to textbooks and materials used with all students) are used when appropriate.
   - Materials are appropriate and interesting.

7. **ACADEMIC ENGAGED TIME:** The student is actively engaged in responding to academic content; the teacher monitors the extent to which the student is actively engaged and re-directs the student when the student is unengaged. This is to be evaluated by taking into account: 4 3 2 1

   Student Involvement
   - The student actively participates in the lesson.
   - Student attention is maintained through appropriate pacing and the provision of opportunities to respond.
   - Questions or probes are directed to the student, and the student gets frequent opportunities to respond.
   - The student spends little time waiting.

   Maintenance of Student Engagement
   - Student activity is monitored.
   - There is an established mechanism for the student to get help if needed.
   - There are established procedures and activities for the student when work is finished early.

— OVER —

Figure 2.2. Continued

8. **INFORMED FEEDBACK:** The student receives relatively immediate and specific information on his/her performance or behavior; when the student makes mistakes, correction is provided. This is to be evaluated by taking into account: 4 3 2 1

   Feedback
   - There is immediate, frequent and explicit feedback about performance or behavior.
   - Feedback emphasizes task-specific praise and encouragement.

   Corrective Procedures
   - Re-explanation is provided:
   - Alternative teaching approaches are used with repeated errors.
   - Modeling of correct processes and reasoning is provided.
   - Prompts and cues are used to reduce errors.

9. **ADAPTIVE INSTRUCTION:** The curriculum is modified to accommodate the student's specific instructional needs. This is to be evaluated by taking into account: 4 3 2 1
   - There is a willingness to modify instruction for the student.
   - There are many instructional options.
   - A variety of teaching methods and materials are used.
   - The student receives additional review and practice in areas of difficulty.
   - There is direct, frequent, continuous monitoring of instruction.

10. **PROGRESS EVALUATION:** There is direct, frequent measurement of the student's progress toward completion of instructional objectives; data on pupil performance and progress are used to plan future instruction. This is to be evaluated by taking into account: 4 3 2 1

    Monitoring Student Progress
    - Instructional objectives and mastery criteria are specified.
    - There is frequent, curriculum-based assessment.
    - Records of student progress are maintained.
    - The student is regularly informed of his/her progress toward mastery of instructional goals.

    Follow-Up Planning
    - The student's errors are systematically analyzed.
    - The student's success rate is compared to the rate of success necessary for mastery of objectives.
    - Data on pupil performance are used to make decisions about whether to review, teach another way, or move to a new skill.

11. **INSTRUCTIONAL PLANNING:** The student's needs have been assessed accurately, and instruction is matched appropriately to the results of the instructional diagnosis. This is to be evaluated by taking into account: 4 3 2 1

    Instructional Diagnosis
    - Effective procedures have been used to ascertain the student's instructional level.
    - The teacher has a good understanding of the student's academic and affective strengths and weaknesses.
    - The curriculum has been task analyzed, and the skills necessary to complete assigned tasks have been identified.
    - The teacher has a good understanding of the complexity of the tasks used with the student and of the skills necessary to complete the tasks successfully.

    Instructional Prescription
    - Instructional goals are appropriate to the level of skill development of the student.
    - Teaching strategies, methods, and materials are matched to the students' interests and level of skill development.
    - Assigned tasks are modified to the extent necessary so that the student experiences success and makes continual progress.
    - Mastery criteria is established.
    - An adequate amount of content is covered.

12. **STUDENT UNDERSTANDING:** The student demonstrates an accurate understanding of what is to be done in the classroom. This is to be evaluated by taking into account: 4 3 2 1
    - The student understands the task directions.
    - The student understands the instructional goals.
    - The student understands the processes required to complete assigned work.

TIES
The Instructional Environment Scale

DATA RECORD FORM

Student _____
Grade _____ Age _____
Date _____
School _____
Setting _____
Teacher _____

SECTION I TIES TEACHER INTERVIEW

1. To what extent was _____'s performance on _____ typical?
   (day)

2. How does your instructional goal for _____ differ from his/her classmates?

3. What are your expectations for _____?
   (Probe for quality of work, classroom participation, task completion, neatness, if assistance is needed.)

4. How do you plan instruction for _____?
   (Probe for strengths, weaknesses, skill level, emotional needs, interests.)

5. How do you determine the appropriate instructional placement for _____?

6. Tell me about _____'s independent assignments.
   (Probe for amount of practice, kind of tasks can handle independently, success rate.)

7. How do you evaluate _____'s progress?
   (Probe for record keeping, decisions about what to teach next, mastery criteria.)

Copyright © 1987 by James E. Ysseldyke and Sandra L. Christenson

Additional copies of this form (#0649) may be ordered from PRO-ED, 5341 Industrial Oaks Blvd. Austin, Texas 78735 USA 512/892-3142

Figure 2.2. Continued

SECTION II EXAMINER OBSERVATION

INSTRUCTIONAL PRESENTATION
- lesson development
- clarity of directions
- checking for student understanding

CLASSROOM ENVIRONMENT
- management
- time-use
- climate

TEACHER EXPECTATIONS

COGNITIVE EMPHASIS

MOTIVATIONAL STRATEGIES

RELEVANT PRACTICE

- opportunity
- task relevance
- materials

ACADEMIC ENGAGED TIME

- student involvement
- maintenance

INFORMED FEEDBACK

- feedback
- corrections

ADAPTIVE INSTRUCTION

PROGRESS EVALUATION

- monitoring
- follow-up planning

Figure 2.2. Continued

SECTION III TIES STUDENT INTERVIEW

1. I want you to tell me what you needed to do on these assignments.

    a. What did your teacher want you to learn?

    b. What did your teacher tell you about why these assignments are important?

    c. What did you have to do?

    d. Show me how you did the work. (Have student explain a sample item.)

2. I am going to ask you several questions. In each case, I want you to tell me your answer by using this scale, where 1 means "not very much" and 4 means "very much."

    a. Sometimes students understand their assignments. Sometimes they don't. Show me how well you understand the assignment.   1 2 3 4

    b. How much did you believe you could do the assignment?   1 2 3 4

    c. How interesting is this work for you?   1 2 3 4

3. Now I have some other questions.

    a. Sometimes students cannot finish their work, and sometimes they have extra time. How much time do you usually get to finish your work: too little (1), just about right (2), or too much (3)?   1 2 3

    b. Does your teacher call on you to answer questions in class: never (1), not much (2), a lot (3)?   1 2 3

4. What does your teacher expect you to do when he or she gives these assignments.

    a. If you are confused?

    b. If you are done with your work?

5. What does your teacher tell you about:

    a. Completing your work? (What happens if your work is not done?)

    b. Getting the answers correct? (What happens if you make mistakes?)

    c. Having neat papers? (What happens if your work is messy?)

6. Student Success Rate:

    a. Number of questions completed _____

    b. Number of correct answers _____

    c. Total number of questions assigned _____

    d. Success rate _____

    e. Kind of errors made by the student _____

TIES
The Instructional Environment Scale

SUMMARY/PROFILE SHEET

James E. Ysseldyke
Sandra L. Christenson

Student _____
Grade _____ Age _____
School _____
Teacher(s) _____
Examiner _____
Referred by _____
Dates of Observation _____
Date of Teacher Interview _____
Date of Student Interview _____

SECTION I   INSTRUCTIONAL RATING PROFILE

How characteristic of the student's instructional environment are indicators of effective instruction in each of the following areas:	Not at All	Not Much	Somewhat	Very Much
1. Instructional Presentation	1	2	3	4
2. Classroom Environment	1	2	3	4
3. Teacher Expectations	1	2	3	4
4. Cognitive Emphasis	1	2	3	4
5. Motivational Strategies	1	2	3	4
6. Relevant Practice	1	2	3	4
7. Academic Engaged Time	1	2	3	4
8. Informed Feedback	1	2	3	4
9. Adaptive Instruction	1	2	3	4
10. Progress Evaluation	1	2	3	4
11. Instructional Planning	1	2	3	4
12. Student Understanding	1	2	3	4

Copyright © 1987 by James E. Ysseldyke and Sandra L. Christenson

Additional copies of this form (#0648) may be purchased from PRO-ED, 5341 Industrial Oaks Blvd. Austin, Texas 78735   512/892-3142

Figure 2.2.   Continued

Appropriateness of LRE Placements 35

SECTION II SETTING

Instructions: Describe the instructional setting. Include information on length of observation, instructional grouping arrangements, instructional content, and number and kinds of tasks occurring. Describe any atypical circumstances.

SECTION III INTERVENTION RECOMMENDATIONS

Instructions: Based on the observation, teacher interview, and student interview, identify areas in which intervention is needed and for each area indicated the action to be taken.

Intervention Needs	Intervention Actions

worked out a schedule so that data for one class per target student were completed each week. Following the directions provided in TIES, Ms. Rice and Mr. Moss recorded anecdotal information on the teacher's instructional presentation, the classroom environment, the teacher's expectations, the cognitive emphasis, and the motivational strategies, if any, that were used during the observation. They recorded this information on the data record forms provided in the TIES instrument. Further information on relevant practice, academic engaged time, informed feedback, adaptive instruction, and progress evaluation was noted. The resource teachers observed an entire 45-minute class period for each teacher and recorded their notes on the inside of the data record form.

Completion of Observations

Immediately following the completion of the observations, the resource teachers began to conduct the interviews. Each target student was interviewed first, with questions such as "What did your teacher want you to learn?" and "What did your teacher tell you about completing your work?" The students' answers were recorded on the data record form. Immediately following each student interview, the teacher was interviewed for approximately 10 minutes (the teachers' classes were directed to their independent seatwork assignments during the interviews). Space was provided on the data record form to record teachers' answers to such questions as "To what extent was the student in question's performance typical?" and "How did you evaluate that student's progress?"

Results

The next step involved scoring the results by completing the instructional rating form and summary profile sheet. It was decided that the resource teachers would also score the results because they were the most familiar with the observations and the interviews. To do this, they judged each of the 12 TIES components on a 4-point Likert-type scale in terms of the degree to which they felt each component was characteristic of the student's instructional environment. Their judgments also were to reflect the data collected through interviews and observations. The 4-point scale used is shown in Table 2.1.

Prior to completing their scoring task, Ms. Rice and Mr. Moss decided to meet in order to review the descriptions of each of the 12 components provided in the appendix of the TIES manual. They also reviewed the critical factors that need to be considered when rating each component. They also planned a practice scoring task by gathering the data for the first student's profile. They believed this would allow them to become comfortable using the rating system and also ensure that they were reasonably consistent in their ratings. The

TABLE 2.1 Percentage TIES Scores for Student Sample

	Similarity to the Student's Instruction			
	Not at All	Not Much	Somewhat	Very Much
1. Instructional presentation	0	60	40	0
2. Classroom environment	0	0	20	80
3. Teacher expectations	0	20	60	20
4. Cognitive emphasis	60	20	20	0
5. Motivational strategies	0	0	40	60
6. Relevant practice	0	0	40	60
7. Academic engaged time	0	0	40	60
8. Informed feedback	0	40	40	20
9. Adaptive instruction	0	0	20	80
10. Progress evaluation	0	40	40	20
11. Instructional planning	0	0	20	80
12. Student understanding	0	60	20	20

ratings (shown in Table 2.1) suggest that, for this target student, classroom strengths centered around a well-managed and supportive classroom environment with a strong academic focus (see items 2, 9, 10, and 11). The areas that needed improvement to encourage more effective mainstreaming were more complete lesson presentations and more checking for student understanding, especially during seatwork (see items 1, 4, 8, and 12).

Focus on Classroom Practices

Because the focus of this evaluation was not on individual students but on classroom practices, the resource teachers combined the data from all target students in the classes to provide a sense of how accommodating the school's instructional environment tended to be for students with diverse special needs. Individual profiles also were made available to teachers to show them how things were going for particular students. After combining the profiles across the five students, the resource teachers developed a chart that used percentages to illustrate the students' instructional profiles as a group.

Interpretation

Upon completion of the exercise of combining the data across students, Ms. Rice and Mr. Moss felt they had a picture of the strengths and weaknesses of the mainstreaming effort at Scottsdale School. They met with the evaluation committee and presented their results. Instructional strengths centered around the following: The observed classrooms were controlled efficiently and effectively; the teachers held realistic, yet high expectations for both the amount and accuracy of work to be completed; most teachers used effective strategies for heightening student interest and effort; most students were given adequate opportunity to practice with appropriate materials; students were engaged actively in responding to academic content; the curriculum was modified in most classes to accommodate specific instructional needs; and student needs usually were assessed accurately. The instructional weaknesses pointed to incomplete lesson presentations with too little checking for student understanding, especially during seatwork. Also, students frequently were not clear on task directions and what was expected of them in the mainstream classes.

Use of the Results

The committee decided to provide feedback to all teachers as a group, with the regular teachers, Ms. Green and Mrs. Sobel, explaining the instructional components that were reviewed. They agreed on intervention needs and decided to meet next week with Dr. Cohen to discuss actions to be taken to improve the school's areas of weakness. Dr. Cohen believed that all of the teachers should feel good about the fact that out of the 12 instructional components only a third were shown to be areas in need of improvement, whereas the rest were considered areas of strength.

Summary of Evaluation Principles

The following important principles should be kept in mind in all evaluations of school programs.

1. Do not attempt to evaluate every aspect of a program at once. Focus the evaluation by selecting a few indicators of quality.
2. When choosing a method of data collection, try to select an alternative that minimizes the burden on those who will be asked to provide information and that can be implemented within your resources and schedule.
3. Whenever appropriate, inform participants of the evaluation goals and allow for voluntary participation. Guarantee confidentiality; if appropriate, provide anonymity.
4. Collect information that will help to identify program strengths and weaknesses and to guide action when improvement is needed.
5. Because TIES uses an ordinal scale, the following characteristics need to be kept in mind: (a) each point is mutually exclusive; (b) the points on the scale are exhaustive; (c) the points on the scale rank from low to high on the dimension of interest; and (d) the intervals between the points on the scale are not equal.

6. If using a standardized instrument, always set aside time prior to data collection to become familiar with the parts of the instrument and appropriate administration procedures.
7. If you are conducting observations or interviews within a classroom, keep everyone who is involved in the process aware of the procedures and the reasons why you are conducting the observations and interviews.

Alternatives to the TIES Strategy

The evaluation team in this example chose to take a rigorous approach to examining the appropriateness of LRE placements. That is, they decided to gather information about the *quality* of their mainstreaming attempts as a measure of the extent to which "school personnel make every effort to serve exceptional students in the least restrictive setting possible." They chose this approach because they wanted a procedure that was both comprehensive and prescriptive. As an alternative, they could have focused their attention on evaluating the extent (or *quantity*) of their mainstreaming efforts. Had they taken this approach, they might have gathered information by reviewing minutes from IEP meetings or reviewing the IEPs themselves, perhaps using some sort of checklist. Information might also have been obtained by surveying teachers about the numbers and types of exceptional children they saw in their classes and the amount of time these youngsters were seen. Although this option would not provide insight as to how responsive regular class settings were to exceptional students' needs, it would provide basic information concerning the extent to which exceptional children were being given access to mainstream settings.

Possible Misinterpretations

As the TIES manual suggests, this instrument is not a teacher evaluation scale. Although the teacher is an essential component of each student's instructional environment, TIES was not designed to be used as a teacher evaluation scale and should not be used as such.

Five children constitute a very small sample of the population, and the picture that their data present may not be a true picture of the entire school. One runs the risk of randomly selecting one or two children who are clearly odd cases and may not depict what most students in the school typically experience. Keep in mind that the data collected from TIES should be used as a general indicator of programmatic strengths and weaknesses. Refer to Chapter 5 of the general guide for more discussion on using the results of a program evaluation.

3
Vignette Three

Satisfaction of Program Participants

Where, What, and Why

The Patricia Holman Middle School, in the town of Rumely, was built in 1965 and has a current enrollment of 515 students in grades 6-8. Originally a neighborhood school in a predominantly white area, the school now is attended by students who are transported by bus from two other neighborhoods in Rumely, resulting in socioeconomic diversity as well as a racial balance of 50% black and 50% white. The neighborhood now is mixed racially, with most parents employed in blue-collar or clerical positions and a few college-educated professionals. Students are bused to Holman from a section of Rumely that is favored by middle-class blacks, as well as another area of town populated by low-income and unemployed residents, also predominantly black.

Jean Stephenson has just accepted the principalship at Holman Middle School and is committed to providing the highest quality education possible for all the students in her new school. Having had several years experience in the classroom before becoming a principal, she is attuned to the needs of teachers and students and quickly has gained the respect and cooperation of her staff in her efforts to improve instructional practices. After much discussion during the first few faculty meetings of the year, it was agreed that program evaluation would be an appropriate vehicle for determining the school's strengths as well as target areas of need and would provide school staff with the information needed to strengthen their instructional program.

The mother of a child with disabilities, Ms. Stephenson is interested particularly in the quality of special education services in Rumely, especially those in her school. She attended the first school-based assessment committee (SBAC) meeting of the year and became concerned about what appeared to be apathy on the part of parents whose children were being served in the resource program. She also was worried about reports of the reluctance of some parents to enroll their children in the program once they qualified.

Lack of Parental Involvement

Cathy Nichols, an experienced resource teacher beginning her second year at Holman, expressed her concern as well, having been frustrated the previous year by lack of parental involvement not only with the process of developing IEPs but also with regard to support at home for the school's efforts to meet students' needs. Her frustration was exacerbated further by the fact that the previous principal at Holman seemed disinterested in the program and did not bother to attend the SBAC meetings. She was delighted that her new principal was very knowledgeable with regard to the needs of students with disabilities and very supportive of her resource program.

Together, Ms. Stephenson and Mrs. Nichols agreed that the delivery of special education services to qualified students of Holman Middle School would be an excellent area of focus for evaluation this year, with particular emphasis on the success of the program from parents' points of view. They shared their ideas with the total faculty at the first faculty meeting, and it was agreed that program evaluation this year would begin with a careful examination of the resource program. Because the SBAC was composed of the school counselor, the speech/language therapist, two classroom teachers, the testing coordinator, the principal, and Mrs. Nichols (who was its chairperson), it was agreed that this group was adequately representative and would be the appropriate group to work with Ms. Stephenson to design the program evaluation plan.

Focus for the Evaluation

Ms. Stephenson explained to her group of evaluators that any project as important as program evaluation would benefit from expert guidance. Referring to the Essential Tools for Educators series, she gave them a copy of both *Evaluating School Programs: An Educator's Guide* and *Special Education Programs: A Guide to Evaluation* and suggested that they review the standards and indicators presented in

Resource A of the latter in developing their evaluation plan. The evaluation committee quickly realized that, although quite a few standards and indicators were included in the resource, they did not feel prepared to embark upon an evaluation of the entire program just yet. Given their specific concerns about parent opinion with regard to the success of the existing program, they decided to begin with Standard 8 ("Students are successful in the special education program").

Collecting Information From Students and Parents

Because both indicators for Standard 8 (Indicators 8.1, "Students and their parents perceive students' participation in the program as positive," and 8.2, "Students and their parents are satisfied with students' progress") involve collecting information from students and from parents, the committee discussed the various ways this might be accomplished. They quickly realized that an appropriate method of data collection could not be selected until after they selected specific evaluation questions to guide their work. (See Chapter 2 of the general guide for a discussion of how to identify evaluation questions.) Ms. Stephenson explained that their evaluation questions would generally fall into two categories: formative (e.g., is the program working as planned? What are the problems? What changes might improve the program?) and summative (e.g., do students and parents perceive the program as being worthwhile?). Committee members then were charged with generating a tentative set of evaluation questions and planning to meet again in 1 week to finalize the list. Their working list of evaluation questions was as follows:

Formative:

1. Do parents feel that test data, placement decisions, and the special needs of their child have been explained adequately to them?
2. Do parents agree with their child's placement?
3. Do parents have confidence in the ability of school personnel to deliver effective services?
4. What changes would parents like to see?
5. What changes would the student like to see?
6. Do parents feel communication between home and school is effective?

Summative:

1. Do parents think the program has made a difference in their child's progress in school?
2. Do students think the program has helped them?
3. Do parents and students feel the program has made a difference in students' self-esteem?

How to Evaluate?

After finalizing the list of evaluation questions, the committee discussed possible alternatives for collecting the data. A telephone survey of parents and students was suggested and discussed. Because this would require the installation of a new telephone and the hiring of additional personnel to conduct the survey, this method was rejected. One group member suggested that they call a meeting of resource parents and students to discuss the program and offer opportunities to express satisfaction or dissatisfaction with the program. This alternative likewise was rejected for several reasons. Mrs. Nichols explained that finding a time that would be convenient for so many people would be virtually impossible, not to mention the fact that her experience with resource parents suggested that attendance at such a meeting would be low and therefore not representative of the intended data source. Another group member noted that such a meeting would not provide anonymity, a factor that most members agreed would be essential for the frank expression of true opinions of both the parents and the students. Agreeing that failure to provide anonymity, or at least confidentiality, would no doubt threaten the validity of their data, the committee came to the conclusion that a questionnaire would be the most appropriate instrument for collecting their data.

Separate Questionnaires

At their next meeting, the evaluation committee began the process of rewriting their evaluation questions into questionnaire items that would allow them to obtain effectively the information they desired from parents and from students. They discussed whether to include questions intended for parents and students on the same questionnaire, asking parents to help their children with their responses. Again concerned about threats to validity, they decided that students should have opportunities to respond separately from their parents. It was agreed that a separate student questionnaire would be designed, with a readability level appropriate to the students' needs. Parent questionnaires would be mailed; student questionnaires would be administered during the school day by the school counselor, Mr. Wilson. Mr. Wilson also offered to be responsible for assembling the data and compiling the results.

The Evaluation Instrument

Mrs. Nichols and Ms. Stephenson offered to generate a first draft of the questionnaires for subsequent revision and/or approval by the evaluation team. They began by reviewing Chapter 3 of *Evaluating School Programs: An Educator's Guide* for guidelines on developing questionnaires. They also consulted Resource B of *Special Education Programs: A Guide to Evaluation* for helpful references to assist them as they were constructing their questionnaire. They chose a Likert-scale format, which offers a set of five choices of levels of agreement or disagreement (plus a sixth option to mark if the question is not applicable). Both positively and negatively worded questions can be used in a Likert format, thereby decreasing the likelihood of a "response set" (i.e., the tendency people sometimes have to mark the same response to a long list of positive statements out of habit). Use of a Likert-scale format would also be more sensitive than a forced-choice scale, where respondents could only agree or disagree with statements. The Likert format would allow respondents to show degrees of agreement or disagreement. Mrs. Nichols and Ms. Stephenson also felt it was important to solicit any comments that parents or students wished to make, so several open-ended items were included at the end of the questionnaires. With only minor revisions, the questionnaires were approved by the committee; the final instruments are represented in Figures 3.1 and 3.2. The letter that accompanied the mailed parent questionnaires is shown in Figure 3.3.

Results

The initial return rate for the parent questionnaire was only 50%, which, although not surprising, caused the evaluation committee some concern. Having anticipated this as a potential problem, the committee numbered each questionnaire and kept on file a list of corresponding parent names so that they could identify nonrespondents. Mrs. Nichols was then able to send reminders to those parents who had not responded, assuring them that their responses would be kept confidential and reminding them that they need not sign the questionnaire. Additional completed questionnaires were received during the following week, bringing the response rate up to a more acceptable 82%. Because of the diligent efforts of the student council members administering the student questionnaire, the response rate for students was 97% (one student moved during the week the questionnaires were administered).

Mr. Wilson summarized the results of the questionnaires. He began with a blank questionnaire and made tally marks to record responses for each item. He then counted the marks in each response category and calculated the corresponding percentages. Recalling that items 5, 6, 11, 14, 18, 20, 23, and 25 were worded negatively, Mr. Wilson reversed the scores when recording responses for these questions. While calculating percentages, he noticed that lower percentages were being recorded consistently for items related to home/school

Please read each statement below and circle the response that best matches your view.

Please answer each question to the best of your knowledge.

Your responses will be kept strictly confidential. A self-addressed, stamped envelope is provided for your convenience. Please respond by Friday, October 3.

1 = Strongly agree
2 = Agree somewhat
3 = Undecided
4 = Disagree somewhat
5 = Strongly disagree
6 = Not applicable

		SA	A	U	D	SD	NA
1.	My child's placement in special education is appropriate.	1	2	3	4	5	6
2.	Results and findings of testing and other diagnostic activities were adequately explained to me.	1	2	3	4	5	6
3.	I was supplied adequate information on the nature of my child's special needs.	1	2	3	4	5	6
4.	I was made aware of my rights as parent of an exceptional child.	1	2	3	4	5	6
5.	Activities in the special education program do not meet my child's needs.	1	2	3	4	5	6
6.	The special education program does not have adequate materials to meet my child's needs.	1	2	3	4	5	6
7.	I am pleased with the number of progress notes I receive from my child's special education teacher.	1	2	3	4	5	6
8.	My child's special education teacher answers my questions quickly and professionally.	1	2	3	4	5	6
9.	I am pleased with the quality of the instructional program provided by my child's special education teacher.	1	2	3	4	5	6
10.	My child's IEP goals are realistic for my child.	1	2	3	4	5	6
11.	My child's IEP does not contain all the goals I feel are important.	1	2	3	4	5	6
12.	I am pleased with the extent my judgments were used in my child's IEP.	1	2	3	4	5	6
13.	I am pleased with the people who are involved in my child's education (teachers, therapists, assistants, administrators).	1	2	3	4	5	6
14.	I am disappointed with the amount of contact I have with my child's special education teacher.	1	2	3	4	5	6
15.	I am pleased with the amount of time my child spends with the special education teacher.	1	2	3	4	5	6
16.	Regularly scheduled school activities and resources (library, music, art, physical education, etc.) are adequately available to my child.	1	2	3	4	5	6
17.	My child should spend more time in the regular classroom.	1	2	3	4	5	6
18.	My child seldom enjoys school.	1	2	3	4	5	6
19.	My child enjoys his/her special program.	1	2	3	4	5	6

Figure 3.1. Parent Questionnaire *(continued)*

	SA	A	U	D	SD	NA
20. My child does not enjoy his/her special program because he/she feels different from children who are not enrolled in a special program.	1	2	3	4	5	6
21. I am pleased with the amount of supplemental activities in which my child participates during the school day (guest speakers, field trips, etc.).	1	2	3	4	5	6
22. I am pleased with my child's transportation to and from school.	1	2	3	4	5	6
23. I am disappointed with the progress made by my child while with the special education teacher.	1	2	3	4	5	6
24. I am pleased with the amount of homework my child brings home from the special education teacher.	1	2	3	4	5	6
25. I disagree with the amount and type of therapy my child receives (speech, physical, occupational).	1	2	3	4	5	6
26. I am pleased with the facility which my child attends.	1	2	3	4	5	6

Overall, are you satisfied with the special education services provided by Holman School for your exceptional child?

Please use the following space to describe any additional comments or concerns you might have with regard to the services your child receives.

DIRECTIONS: Please answer each question by drawing a circle around the word that best matches how you feel.

1. I like going to school.
   never   not often   sometimes   usually   always
2. I am a good student.
   no   sometimes   yes
3. I do not like going to special classes.
   never   not often   sometimes   usually   always
4. I would like to spend more time in my special class.
   no   yes
5. My special teacher helps me when I have a problem.
   never   sometimes   always
6. I think my special classes have helped me to improve on my other school work.
   none   a little   some   a lot
7. I would like to spend more time in my regular class.
   no   yes
8. I have too much homework in my special class.
   no   sometimes   yes
9. I have too much homework in my regular class.
   no   sometimes   yes
10. I want to continue going to special classes.
    no   yes

What else would you like to tell us about your special classes?

Figure 3.2. Student Questionnaire

Satisfaction of Program Participants 47

> Dear Parents,
>
> The Patricia Holman Middle School faculty and staff are committed to providing the highest quality education possible for all the students enrolled in our school. We are especially interested in your views concerning the quality of our program for children with special needs. We are asking that you, as parents of an exceptional child, respond to the enclosed questionnaire so that we can better assess our areas of strength and target our areas of need. Your input is important to us in our efforts to strengthen our instructional services for exceptional students.
>
> Please be assured that your responses to the questionnaire will be kept strictly confidential. We would appreciate your returning the questionnaire by October 3. A self-addressed, stamped envelope is included for your convenience.
>
> Sincerely,
>
> Jean S. Stephenson, Principal
> Patricia Holman Middle School

Figure 3.3. Parent Letter

communication on the parent questionnaire. He therefore decided to arrange the items into broad categories so that interpretation of the data would be easier. For the student questionnaire, Mr. Wilson simply used a blank questionnaire for his summary. He presented the results to the committee in the form shown in Table 3.1 and Figure 3.4.

Results of Parent Questionnaires

Interpretation

The results of the parent questionnaires seemed to indicate general satisfaction with the quality of special education services at Holman Middle School. Consistently positive responses were obtained for those items relating to the instructional program. Of the parent respondents, 84% agreed with their child's placement, 91% were pleased with his or her progress, and 94% indicated that their child enjoyed going to special classes. On the other hand, responses to items relating to home/school communication were generally negative, with the exception of item 4 (awareness of parental rights). Most responses (88%) to the final question (regarding overall satisfaction) were positive.

Additional comments from parents were few and varied widely in scope. All but two were positive in nature, and both negative comments concerned the amount of homework the parents' child brought home, not from resource class, but from the regular classroom

1. I like going to school.
never	not often	sometimes	usually	always
0%	6%	22%	66%	6%

2. I am a good student.
no	sometimes	yes
78%	16%	6%

3. I do not like going to special classes.
never	not often	sometimes	usually	always
34%	44%	22%	0%	0%

4. I would like to spend more time in my special class.
no	yes
9%	91%

5. My special teacher helps me when I have a problem.
no	sometimes	yes
0%	9%	91%

6. I think my special classes have helped me to improve on my other school work.
none	a little	some	a lot
0%	6%	19%	75%

7. I would like to spend more time in my regular class.
no	yes
12%	88%

8. I have too much homework in my special class.
no	sometimes	yes
91%	6%	3%

9. I have too much homework in my regular class.
no	sometimes	yes
3%	9%	88%

10. I want to continue going to special classes.
no	yes
3%	97%

Figure 3.4. Summary of Student Questionnaires

teacher (e.g., class work the child did not finish because of leaving the room for special classes).

The results of the student questionnaire were almost entirely positive. Ninety-seven percent of the students responded that they would like to continue going to resource classes. Negative responses tended to relate to self-esteem (item 2) and homework (item 9). Additional comments from students were largely of two types: "Mrs. Nichols is very nice," and "I like using the computers in Mrs. Nichols' room."

TABLE 3.1 Summary of Parent Questionnaire

Percentage of responses by category	SD	D	U	A	SA	NA
Instructional Program						
5. Activities meet needs	03	09	09	32	47	00
6. Adequate materials	00	12	03	69	16	00
9. Quality of instruction	00	03	03	35	59	00
10. Realistic IEP goals	00	00	06	50	44	00
11. Goals are important	03	03	03	44	47	00
13. Pleased with people	00	00	00	16	84	00
15. Time spent in resource	00	16	03	09	50	22
24. Resource homework	00	16	03	09	50	22
25. Therapists	00	06	03	47	16	28
Home/School Communication						
2. Adequate explanation	03	54	06	25	06	06
3. Adequate information	03	54	06	25	09	03
4. Parental rights	03	06	00	75	13	03
7. Notes received	48	34	03	09	06	00
8. Teacher answers questions	22	53	13	09	03	00
12. IEP input	06	25	25	31	13	00
14. Amount of contact	25	63	06	06	00	00
Other						
1. Agree with placement	04	06	06	25	59	00
16. Other school activities	09	40	19	16	16	00
17. Time in regular class	16	06	06	09	06	00
18. Child enjoys school	03	03	00	66	28	00
19. Child enjoys resource	00	03	03	22	72	00
20. Child feels different	13	53	09	19	06	00
21. Supplemental activities	16	59	03	16	06	00
22. Transportation	03	03	00	59	22	13
23. Progress in resource	00	03	06	38	53	00
26. Facility	06	25	09	47	13	00

Use of Results

Results of the survey indicated a need to revise the homework policy for exceptional students at Holman Middle School. This was reflected in both the parent and student responses. As a result of the student questionnaire, issues related to enhancing self-esteem also emerged as an area requiring attention. In addition, it seemed clear from the parents' responses that many of them would appreciate better and more frequent communication with school personnel regarding their exceptional child. After much discussion of the ramifications of these results, the committee produced the following list of recommendations:

1. The school-based assessment committee will meet with teachers at each grade level in order to:
   a. discuss scheduling of the school day, with efforts made to minimize the impact of the student's being absent from the classroom for part of the school day
   b. establish homework policy that is reasonable for students with special needs
   c. discuss the ways in which school personnel can have a positive impact on the child's self-esteem
2. Specialists will design an appropriate format for communicating exceptional students' progress to parents on a monthly basis. These reports will be mailed to exceptional students' parents.
3. Three activities (e.g., open house, a holiday party, a spring picnic) will be scheduled each year to foster the involvement of exceptional students' parents in school activities and to enhance communication between home and school.
4. Parents of exceptional students will be invited to at least two parent/teacher conferences per year with the resource teacher and other specialists, as well as the classroom teacher, in attendance.
5. The home/school coordinator will be contacted to help provide transportation for parents who need it in order to attend the conferences.

Summary of Evaluation Principles

1. Do not attempt to evaluate every aspect of a program at once. Focus the evaluation by selecting a few indicators of quality from the list in Resource A.
2. When choosing a method of data collection, try to select an alternative that minimizes the burden on those who will be asked to provide information.
3. Remember that evaluation often requires hard judgments and negative responses that people might be reluctant to express. If at all possible, design the evaluation in ways that permit those who provide information to preserve their privacy. Always guarantee confidentiality. If possible, provide anonymity.
4. Whenever possible, collect information in ways that give every member of the group of interest an opportunity to respond. Plan the evaluation so that participation is of minimal inconvenience to the respondents.
5. Ask questions your information providers are able to answer. Keep in mind the readability level of the instruments you use to seek information and the skills of those responding.
6. Collect information that will help to identify areas of program success and weakness. The information gained should guide remedial action when improvement is needed.

7. Whenever possible, seek redundant information. Ask several questions about each important evaluation issue, and seek information from more than one source.

Alternatives to the Survey Strategy

As discussed earlier, alternative data collection strategies for this evaluation include telephone surveys and group meetings. Interviews would also be a possible choice. In the interest of providing anonymity and minimizing respondent burden, which were essential components in this evaluation, this committee chose to mail questionnaires to parents.

Students might have been assisted by their parents, or by teachers, but assistance from other students would seem to decrease the likelihood of eliciting only "socially acceptable" responses (as opposed to those that accurately reflected the students' opinions).

Possible Misinterpretations

A most important caution with regard to the interpretation of these data concerns the extent to which the 82% of parents who responded to the survey were truly representative of all parents of the schools' exceptional students. (See Chapter 3 of the general guide for comments on acceptable rates of return for questionnaires.) The evaluator must seriously consider the many possible reasons for the lack of response by the remaining 18%. Did they not respond because they were disinterested? Angry with school personnel? Angry with the resource teacher? Limited in their own reading and writing skills? Making judgments on questions such as these is difficult at best, but one cannot assume that those who did respond speak for those who did not. It is sometimes possible to examine questions like these by comparing the known characteristics of respondents and nonrespondents (grade level of parents' child, ethnicity of child, child's exceptionality, etc.). When large differences are found, additional efforts to secure information from nonrespondents—perhaps telephone follow-up in this case—are warranted.

4 Vignette Four

What's Going On in Classrooms?

Where, What, and Why

The Lafayette County School District is located approximately 25 miles southwest of a large metropolitan area. It covers the largest geographic area in its state. The district has 6 high schools, 6 middle schools, and 14 elementary schools. Schools are spread in clusters across the county according to feeder patterns; several elementary schools feed into each middle school, and each middle school feeds into a high school. Although schools in the clusters are relatively close to one another, the clusters themselves are not. As a result, considerable diversity is found across clusters of schools. Some are located in very rural settings, whereas others are situated in more populated areas. The schools serve families with a wide range of socioeconomic levels.

Where Improvements Are Needed

Nine years ago, Dr. Kenneth Horn became the director of exceptional children's services for the Lafayette County School District. At that time, he and his staff of five disability area supervisors began working with school personnel to implement an ongoing program of evaluation across the county's special education programs. This was motivated, in part, by the differences that Dr. Horn, his disability area supervisors, and the building principals observed among special education programs operating in different schools. Some programs appeared to be working well, but others seemed to be less effective.

Dr. Horn wanted to find out where improvements were needed and what could be done to strengthen the district's programs.

Early evaluation efforts focused on such issues as determining the extent to which his special education teachers needed training in particular areas and assessing the availability and quality of program resources at each school. Later, evaluation efforts moved beyond such basic concerns to include issues like evaluating the impact of newly instituted "assistance teams" on student referral rates and the accuracy of teacher referrals. In each instance, Dr. Horn, his staff, and the building principals used outcomes from their evaluations to make adjustments in existing programs or to guide the development of new programs. As a result, the quality and consistency of the county's special education programs gradually improved over the years.

Dr. Horn and his staff met with the special education teachers and their building principals toward the end of the school year to begin planning their next evaluation project. At the meeting, he suggested the possibility of taking on a fairly ambitious project, that of studying the nature of the instructional programs being provided for exceptional children. The goal of the evaluation would be to determine the extent to which elements of sound practice for special education were reflected in the school system's classrooms.

After considerable discussion, the group decided that although their task could be considerably more complicated than previous evaluation efforts, results of such an evaluation would prove enormously helpful in directing staff development and program planning activities. A carefully developed evaluation plan would allow them to identify important elements of effective instructional practice that were missing or being implemented poorly in classrooms and would point to specific improvements in instructional programs that should be made. Moreover, the group felt they were ready to attempt such a project. They had been participating routinely in evaluation activities for some time now and were gaining confidence in their ability to conduct effective evaluations.

Focus for the Evaluation

Dr. Horn told the group that the type of evaluation they had in mind could require fairly extensive resources. In view of this, he suggested that the evaluation should take place over an extended period of time. The group developed a plan whereby an evaluation team made up of Dr. Horn, his staff of disability area specialists, and five volunteer special education teachers would concentrate initially on studying limited aspects of instructional programs and do so in a small number of schools.

It was decided that the evaluation team would meet periodically throughout the summer to develop their evaluation plan. The special education teachers on the team would be compensated for their time by using funds from Dr. Horn's discretionary budget. All other members of the team were employed on a 12-month basis and would not require additional compensation.

Student On-Task Behavior

The evaluation team began their first meeting by reviewing the list of standards and indicators of quality of special education programs contained in Resource A of this guide. Of particular interest to them were the indicators listed under Standard 10 ("Quality special education programs emphasize principles of effective practice widely held to be applicable across grade levels and areas of exceptionality"). Dr. Horn suggested they select Indicator 10.5 ("Classrooms are characterized by high rates of student time on task") as a starting point for the evaluation. He knew there was extensive research evidence that showed students' time on task was one of the most critical factors contributing to their growth in achievement. He felt that outcomes from this project would be extremely valuable in showing teachers where improvements could be made, particularly if the evaluation provided some insight as to how children were spending their time (i.e., the nature of their activities). After Dr. Horn recognized that this evaluation focus would demand substantial staff investment, the evaluation team remained committed to their goal, as they felt the end result would be of sufficient value to warrant their efforts. They did, however, agree to limit the project initially to classrooms serving mildly to moderately handicapped students operating in the county's 14 elementary schools. Subsequent efforts would focus on classes at the middle and high school levels, as well as on programs for the severely and profoundly handicapped. They also decided it would be useful to seek some expert guidance from within the district to assist them in their evaluation, because no one in the group felt they had sufficient experience in conducting this type of evaluation. Dr. Horn indicated he would ask Paul Walters from the district's central office evaluation staff to serve as an expert consultant.

How to Evaluate?

Having agreed to work with the group, Mr. Walters joined Dr. Horn and the evaluation team at their next meeting, when they then considered how they would go about assessing Indicator 10.5. The focus of their discussion was on identifying the types of information they would need to gather and sources that could provide such information (see Chapter 3 of the general guide for a summary of common information sources and data collection methods).

Direct Observation of Classroom Activities

It was agreed that the evaluation question they sought to answer was, "How are mildly to moderately handicapped children spending their class time, especially with respect to their rates of on-task behavior?" In order to gather data to answer this question, the evaluation team discussed the possibility of systematically reviewing teachers' plan books and asking them to keep time logs. This approach was rejected, however, because it was agreed that what actually occurred in classrooms (i.e., how children spent their time) could differ significantly from what was intended (i.e., what was shown in the plan books and logs). According to Mr. Walters, the best way to find out what actually was occurring in classrooms might be to do some form of direct observation of classroom activities, an idea that quickly was endorsed by the group. It was suggested that perhaps this could be done by training teachers to do periodic observations in their own classrooms and to provide written summaries of the outcomes. After some discussion, however, this plan was rejected. It was felt that teachers might have a difficult time being unbiased in reporting what they observed. In addition, the evaluation team felt that because they wanted to obtain a rather detailed picture of what was happening in classes, a more extensive system of observation would be needed. Teachers simply wouldn't have the time to use such a system and also fulfill their teaching responsibilities.

Having decided to gather information through observation, the evaluation team still had to answer several important questions. How extensive an observation system would be needed to provide a clear sense of how children spent their class time? How many times and for what duration would classes have to be observed to obtain such information? Who would do the observations? What other constraints, if any, should be considered?

Paul Walters suggested that in order to select an appropriate observation system, he would obtain several books from the district's professional library. He chose introductory research texts that would provide the group with information about conducting observation studies and developing observation systems, in addition to more advanced texts that focused on classroom observation. He also suggested that the evaluation team examine Chapter 3 of *Evaluating School Programs: An Educator's Guide* and Resource B of this guide for sources of additional information on observation systems. From these sources, the team learned that the continuum of observation methods ranges from very informal to highly structured. The team found that informal methods, although typically easier to use than formal ones, would not provide very specific information. The team also learned that although formal observation is more complex and time-consuming, it usually provides more accurate and detailed results. Because they not only were interested in judging the incidence of students' on-task behavior in classes but also wanted to learn how students were spending their time, the team decided that a formal observation system was needed.

Use of a Coding Instrument

From their readings, the evaluation team learned that two types of formal observation instruments might suit their needs. First, they could develop an on-the-spot checklist that would permit observers to record the presence, absence, or frequency of certain targeted behaviors. The checklist could also be designed to permit recording of the duration of behaviors. The team rejected this idea, however, when they learned that checklists provide little insight into the precise form of behaviors, something that was of particular interest in the evaluation. Instead, the team decided to use a system involving coded behavior records. This would allow observers to record in detail the range of activities that occurred within a given time period. The team understood that this could be a difficult observation method to use, but all members of the evaluation team agreed that this was the best way they could accurately secure the information they wanted with acceptable accuracy and detail.

Next, the evaluation team members turned their attention to determining how many observations of classes should be made and how long each should last. They realized that the length of time could vary, because there was no standard time frame for conducting observations. They didn't want to tax their resources any more than necessary. But they also knew their time samples would have to be long enough and occur frequently enough to provide an accurate picture of students' typical behaviors.

It was decided that each observation should last for 40 minutes. This would allow observers to accommodate programs operated in self-contained classes as well as in resource rooms, where the typical class length was 40 minutes. The team also decided that observations would occur six times during the first 9-week grading period. An observation schedule would be drawn up for each classroom, taking care to space them out over the grading period so as to provide the most representative picture of classroom events. The schedule would also be designed to show different times of the day, again so that a representative picture could be obtained.

The team members then turned their attention to deciding who would do the observing. They realized that school personnel already had more than their share of responsibilities and that adding another might not be greeted with enthusiasm. Two strategies were discussed. One was to have the disability area specialists do the observations. It was agreed that although this was a possibility, the extensiveness of the task might make this solution impractical. Each of the 14 schools had one special education class, and each would have to be observed a total of six times, resulting in a grand total of 84 observations across schools. Thus each of the five supervisors would have to complete approximately 18 observations during the course of the grading period. All agreed that this would be quite difficult to accomplish.

Strategy number two was to try to identify someone within each school who could conduct the observations in that building, someone who might get something out of doing so. It was suggested that because each school had a counselor, and because counselors play an important role in programming for exceptional children, there might be real value in having counselors do the observations. This would give them an opportunity to learn much about the school's children with special needs and about the special education program itself. Such insight would be of value to counselors in making referrals, participating on assessment teams, and working with special students and their teachers. Moreover, using the counselors as observers would make the task much more feasible, because each would only have to complete six observations over a 9-week grading period. In addition, it would free the disability area specialists to assume other critical responsibilities, such as training the observers and monitoring their reliability.

Dr. Horn met with the building principals to discuss the possibility of having counselors complete the observations. He described the relative merits of having counselors involved, discussed the alternative strategy that had been considered, and pointed out the differences in time commitment it would involve. He also pointed out the ongoing value of training counselors to complete structured observations in terms of assisting them in carrying out their routine responsibilities. All of the building principals endorsed his request.

Use of the SOBR System

Observation Instrument

When they first decided to use an observation system involving coded behavior records, the evaluation team members tried to locate a system that would meet their needs by looking in several books on school program evaluation and searching for examples of evaluation studies that might have used such a system. Although they did not find a system that could be used as written, they were able to locate one that could be adapted to meet their needs. In searching for examples to guide the team, Paul Walters had located a study of reading instruction for students with learning disabilities that used a highly developed observation system called Student Observation of Beginning Reading (SOBR; see Leinhardt & Seewald, 1980, in Resource B). Although the system was designed primarily to describe in detail the reading behaviors of students, it could accommodate a full range of activities occurring within classroom settings, using students, teachers, and instructional aides as targets. It was agreed that the SOBR system, with some modification, could be used in the current evaluation.

As a first step toward modifying the SOBR system, the evaluation team decided to focus on observing students only, and not their teachers or instructional aides. This made sense, because the evaluation question was related to how students spent their time in special education classes. Next, the team members turned their attention to adapting the coding system used to describe observed behaviors. It was clear to everyone that, in some respects, the SOBR system was far more detailed than it needed to be for their purposes. At Paul Walters's suggestion, the team decided to collapse some of the codes to reflect broader categories of behavior, thereby making the system more manageable. For example, rather than using the full range of codes available to describe the nature of students' academic behaviors, the team decided to collapse these into a single code that would indicate student participation in any type of academic task. At this point, the team members also identified SOBR codes and categories of behavior that would not require any modification and those that could be eliminated completely. For example, they decided to eliminate codes that would tell whether students were working alone or with a partner, as they felt their evaluation did not require such information.

Using the SOBR system as a guide, the team agreed to use the small set of behavior categories shown in Table 4.1 and to adopt the symbol codes and operational definitions provided.

Once the team members finished adapting the coding system, they turned their attention to the observation procedure. It was decided that few modifications in the suggested procedures for using the SOBR system would be needed. Observers would be using a procedure whereby each student would be observed for 10 seconds during a 5-minute cycle. The cycle would be repeated every 5 minutes until 40 minutes had passed. As the team members generated their plan, they prepared the observers' recording sheet shown in Figure 4.1, using the SOBR system as a guide.

According to their plan, each observer would prepare for a scheduled observation by completing the identification information on the top of the recording sheet. This would include listing the names of all students down the left-hand side of the form and indicating, in 5-minute increments, the time cycle for each observation period. That is, if the observation was scheduled to begin at 9:00 in the morning, this would be the first notation entered in the time-cycle space. The next spaces would then be marked 9:05, 9:10, and so on until all spaces had been filled, thereby covering a 40-minute class period.

Observers were to use a stopwatch to begin the observation at the designated time. They would then watch the first student on the list for 10 seconds, code the behavior of that student in the next 5 seconds, then use the next 5 seconds to locate the second student. This procedure would be repeated until all students listed were observed, completing an observation cycle. The observer would then wait for his

TABLE 4.1 Behavior Categories and Codes for the SOBR System

Category	Symbol	Behavior
Academic	A	Target student is engaged in an academic instructional activity
Academic Other	AO	Target student is engaged in an instructional activity that is not primarily academic in its focus.
Off-Task	/	Target student is *supposed* to be engaged in an activity but is not actively engaged. This code is given in conjunction with the A and AO codes and would be written as A̸ or A̸O̸.
Waiting	W	Target student is waiting for someone or something in order to continue his or her work. The student needs assistance or materials.
Management	M	Target student is engaged in activities related to preparing for, carrying out, or completing instructional tasks, such as getting materials or sharpening pencils.
Out of Room	X	Target student has left the classroom or is absent.

or her stopwatch to signal the onset of the next 5-minute increment as shown across the top of the recording form. At that time, the observer would initiate a second observation cycle, beginning with the first student listed and continuing until all had been observed. The sequence would be repeated eight times.

For training purposes, the team created the example of a completed observation record form shown in Figure 4.2. Identification information has been marked, and student names have been listed down the left column. The second column shows that the observer began watching the first student, John J., at exactly 10:00. The code entered for John indicates that he was observed to be engaged actively in an academic instructional task for at least the majority of the 10 seconds the observer watched his behavior. This was also true for the second student, Susan. The code shown for the third student shows that although she had an academic assignment, she was not actively engaged in it. The fourth student was observed to be completing an academically related assignment, whereas the fifth was engaged in some form of management activity. Completion of a full observation cycle for this group of students would take 1 minute and 40 seconds (i.e., a total of 20 seconds per student). The observer, therefore, waited 3 minutes and 20 seconds before beginning the next cycle at 10:05, as indicated at the top of the third column.

Training of Observers

On the first of three staff development days held just prior to the opening of the school year, members of the evaluation team and the building principals met with the counselors who were to be involved in the project. Dr. Horn explained the purpose of the project and provided an overview of the counselors' role. In so doing, he described a

Observer: _____ Date: _____
School: _____ Start Time: _____
Teacher: _____ End Time: _____

Time Cycle Increments

Student											Notes/Comments
1.											
2.											
3.											
4.											
5.											
6.											
7.											
8.											
9.											
10.											
11.											
12.											

Figure 4.1. Blank Observation Record Form

Observer: Smith　　　　　　　　　　　　　　　　　Date: 9-27-90
School: Liberty　　　　　　　　　　　　　　　　Start Time: 10:00
Teacher: P. Charles　　　　　　　　　　　　　　End Time: 10:40

Time Cycle Increments

Student	10:00	10:05	10:10	10:15	10:20	10:25	10:30	10:35	Notes/Comments
1. John J.	A	A	A	W	W	AO	X	M	
2. Susan P.	A	A	A	A	A	A	AO	M	
3. Kathy K.	A	A	A	A	A	M	AØ	M	
4. Earl O.	AO	AØ	AØ	M	M	A	A	W	
5. Peter M.	M	A	W	A	A	A	AØ	M	
6.									
7.									
8.									
9.									
10.									
11.									
12.									

Figure 4.2. Completed Observation Record Form

number of steps that would be taken to make certain the project did not become too burdensome for the counselors. For example, he indicated that the evaluation team had taken care to locate and adapt an observation method that would not require extensive training. The evaluation team would teach the counselors how to use the method during the next two staff development days and provide them with ample opportunities to practice using it. Then, a team member would assist each counselor in practicing with the method during the first week of school. All necessary materials would be provided directly to each school throughout the first grading period, and the disability area specialists would be responsible for collecting observation forms on an ongoing basis. The specialists also would be responsible for summarizing the observation data and preparing it for interpretation and presentation.

The evaluation team knew that if they were to get the best possible information from the observations, it was essential that the observers be well trained. To address this concern, they had developed a set of videotaped segments in classrooms. The tapes focused on individual students in the manner required by the observation system.

The team began training by introducing the counselors to the observation system, recording form, and time-cycle procedures. The counselors were then shown the first segment of a training tape and asked to start their stopwatches along with the trainers. Everyone was to code behaviors simultaneously. Initially, the tape was stopped after every 5-minute cycle so that the consistency of coding could be checked, definitions clarified, and unexpected events discussed. Gradually, the length of practice cycles was extended until the group completed enough tapes to feel confident. Practice occurred over the remainder of the day and for a portion of the next.

Training was to continue on an individual basis during the first two weeks of school, when the disability area specialists would complete a practice observation with each counselor in the actual classrooms to be studied. This strategy would allow continued clarification of the system and would provide additional information on observer reliability. The plan called for those who did not obtain a reasonable level of consistency with the trainer to be given additional practice prior to actual data collection. The team felt that another benefit of providing at least one training session in actual classrooms was that it would begin to acclimate teachers and students to having observers in their room.

Reliability

The purpose of systematically training observers was to ensure that all observers were using the same system, rules, and definitions of codes. In this way, data collected in different classrooms by different observers could be assumed to have consistent meaning. In this same vein, Paul Walters suggested that the team should devise a system for monitoring the reliability of observers throughout the data collection phase to ensure that there was no degradation in observer performance. After consulting several sources like those described in Chapter 3 of the general guide of this series, it was decided that observer reliability could be monitored by having disability area specialists accompany each observer on two of their scheduled classroom observations during the 9-week period. As with the training phase, each area specialist would complete the observation simultaneously with the regular observer to whom he or she was assigned, resulting in two sets of observation data that could be compared. The team decided that the rate of agreement between observers should be at least 90% for the results to be considered reliable. In the event this level of reliability was not met, additional training would be provided before the remaining observations were completed.

Results

As pointed out previously, plans called for counselors to deliver their observation forms to the disability specialists on an ongoing basis. The specialists and the remaining members of the evaluation team were then responsible for translating the coded records into an interpretable form. The team began this process by developing the data summary forms shown in Figures 4.3 and 4.4. The form shown in Figure 4.3 would permit them to collapse information obtained across the six observations completed at each school, resulting in a composite picture for each classroom. The form shown in Figure 4.4 would permit them to create a similar composite across observations for individual students in each classroom.

To complete the form shown in Figure 4.3, the evaluation team simply took one of the observation records turned in for Ms. Evans's resource classroom at Crossroads School and counted the number of times each code appeared. The information was recorded in the second column of the summary form as shown in the example. The procedure was then repeated until all codes from the six observations completed in Ms. Evans's resource classroom were recorded in the second column. Next, the number of hatch marks recorded for each code category in the second column was placed in the third column of the form to show the total number of times a category of behavior was observed across all observations in the classroom. This number was then translated to a percentage and recorded in the fourth column of the form using the following steps:

1. The number of observation cycles completed on each record form (i.e., 8) was multiplied by the number of students in Ms. Evans's class to show the total number of observation cells per record form. This resulted in a total number of 40 observation cells per record

Observer: _Dalton_
Classroom: _C. Evans_
School: _Crossroads_
Total Observations: _240_

Code	Summary of Occurences	Total Occurences	Percentage of Total Occurrences
A	//// ///	113	47
A	//// //// //// //// ///	19	8
AO	//// //// //// //// //// //// //// //// ////	48	20
AO	//// //// ////	14	6
W	//// //// //// //// //	14	6
M	//// //// //// ////	22	9
X		10	4

Figure 4.3. Data Summary Form

Observer: __Dalton__
Classroom: __C. Evans__
Target Student: __Tony__

School: __Crossroads__
Total Observations: __48__

Code	Summary of Occurences	Total Occurences	Percentage of Total Observations
A	//// //// //// /	16	33
A̶	////	4	8
AO	//// //	8	17
AØ	//	2	4
W	//// /	6	13
M	//// ////	10	21
X	//	2	4

Figure 4.4. Student Data Summary Form

form, because 5 students attended her resource class during the time targeted for completing the observations.

2. The number of observation cells per record form (i.e., 40) was then multiplied by the number of observations completed in Ms. Evans's classroom (i.e., 6) to show the total number of observation cells contained on all the record forms gathered in her class. This resulted in a total of 240 observation cells across the six observations.

3. Numbers shown in the third column of the form were then converted to percentages by dividing them by 240. For example, the total number of occurrences for the "A" code was 113; when this number is divided by 240, it represents 47% of all observations recorded in Ms. Evans's class.

A similar procedure was followed to complete Figure 4.4, which was designed to provide information on the behavior of individual students. The evaluation team went back through the six observation records for each classroom and counted the number of times each code appeared for each student. This information was recorded in the second and third columns of the form, as shown in the example for Tony presented in Figure 4.4. These totals then were converted to percentages and recorded in the fourth column by multiplying the number of cycles per observation form (i.e., 8) by the number of observations per classroom (i.e., 6) for a grand total of 48 observations. Each of the totals recorded in the third column was then divided by 48 to obtain the percentages.

Summarizing the Results

The evaluation team's next step was to present results from the data summary forms in a manner that could be interpreted easily (see Chapter 4 of the general guide for discussion of various ways of organizing data). At Paul Walters's suggestion, the group decided to illustrate the findings in the form of bar graphs such as the one shown in Figure 4.5, which represents a 40-minute class period and shows the percentage of time that students typically spent engaged in various activities during that period. It was reasoned that bar graphs were a good choice because they would demonstrate the results clearly in a visual form that readily illustrated contrasts and areas of relative emphasis. Also, Paul Walters indicated that although the graphs could be developed by hand, a simple microcomputer program that would produce the graphs was available in the district office (see Resource B).

A set of bar graphs was made to illustrate results for each of the classrooms. The sample graph presented in Figure 4.5 shows that students in this classroom demonstrated relatively high rates of on-task behavior when completing both academic and academically related instructional tasks. It also shows that the teacher of this class appeared to assign almost twice as many academic as academically

What's Going On in Classrooms? 67

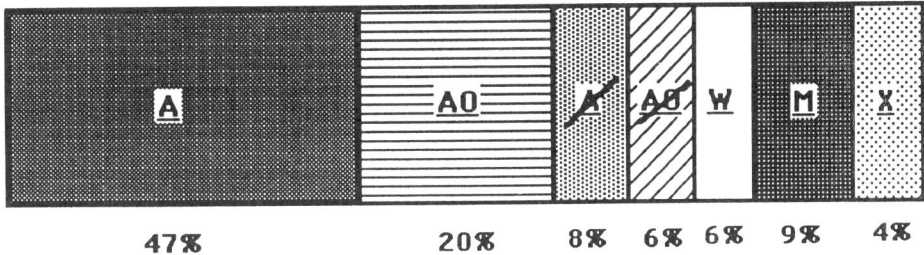

Figure 4.5. Cumulative Percentage of Codes Recorded by Category

related activities. Although the graph shows a relatively small percentage of time being lost to management tasks and waiting, the percentages shown in these categories are noteworthy when combined with the percentages of off-task behavior shown. Taken as a whole, these categories account for 29% of students' time in a typical 40-minute class period.

A second set of graphs like the one shown in Figure 4.5 was made for each teacher, summarizing the results for each student in his or her class. It was felt that this set of graphs would be especially useful in helping teachers consider instructional modifications on an individual basis.

Interpretation

The evaluation team's analysis of the outcomes across classrooms revealed a pattern quite similar to the one reflected in the sample graph presented in Figure 4.5. It was found that classes reflected generally adequate rates of on-task behavior, with students typically engaged in more academic tasks than academically related ones. Unfortunately, the team also found that students in these classrooms spent an inordinate amount of time engaged in management tasks, such as getting books or paper, sharpening pencils, or putting materials away. Their results also showed that additional student time was being lost waiting for either teacher assistance, materials, or directions.

Results for individual students were marked to indicate areas of concern so that subsequent teacher interventions could be as individualized as possible.

Use of Results

Dr. Horn and his evaluation team shared the results of the evaluation with the building principals and special education teachers in several ways. Counselors who participated in the project were also included. Initially, he presented an oral overview of results during a staff development day held late in the school year. He used an overhead transparency that showed 12 composite graphs, none of which was labeled by school. Dr. Horn began by pointing out the consistency of the pattern noted across the graphs with respect to specific areas of strength and weakness. He then indicated that he planned to use the results to design a series of workshops for the next year that might be of interest to teachers. The workshops would be targeted at teaching them simple strategies to help reduce the amount of students' time being lost to instructional management concerns and waiting.

Dr. Horn told the group that results would also be made available to them in the form of a brief written report that summarized findings for their school. He noted that these reports would provide individual teachers with specific information about their own classrooms. He then showed several anonymous examples of the student summary graphs that had been prepared and indicated that similar graphs would be included in the written summary materials provided for each teacher. Dr. Horn's presentation was followed by discussion of how the student graphs could be used to guide individualized changes in classrooms.

Summary of Evaluation Principles

This example illustrated several important principles (listed below) that should be kept in mind when evaluating school programs, particularly when the evaluation will involve observations.

1. Do not attempt to evaluate every aspect of a program at once. Focus the evaluation by selecting a few indicators of quality, such as those shown on the list presented in Resource A.
2. When choosing a method of data collection, try to select an alternative that minimizes the burden on those who will be asked to provide information. Although the type of observation system shown in the example requires an extensive commitment of resources, it was organized so as to distribute the burden in a reasonable way among staff members who would likely learn from the observation experience.
3. When developing an observation system, great care should be taken to define behaviors and codes operationally in clear, explicit terms.
4. When a coding system is used, it is helpful to keep the number of codes as small and manageable as possible.
5. Care should be taken in developing an observation sampling plan. It is essential that the plan provide sufficient information to allow accurate conclusions to be drawn. What constitutes an adequate

length of time for observations and number of observations will vary depending on what is being studied.
6. Recording sheets should be designed with an eye toward readily decoding and interpreting results.
7. Develop a clearly thought-out plan for training observers, one that gradually introduces them to the observation system and allows plenty of time for practice. Observers should not collect data until they have demonstrated an appropriate level of consistent performance based on reliability checks against a standard. Reliability checks should also occur periodically throughout data collection so as to monitor observers' performance levels.
8. It is not uncommon for individuals to feel uncomfortable about being observed, particularly when observation first begins. To address this concern, it is sometimes helpful to do a practice observation prior to initiating actual data collection.
9. Although it is difficult to design evaluations involving observations in ways that permit privacy, steps should be taken to guarantee confidentiality and, if possible, anonymity. You'll notice that, in this example, results were shared widely without reference to specific schools or classrooms.

Alternatives to the Observation Strategy

Because the focus of the evaluation was on describing how students in special education classes spent their time, some form of observation was the obvious choice to address this concern. Although the evaluation team considered several observation methods, none of these alternatives would have been as suitable as the approach they used. The team's approach provided a reasonably accurate picture of students' engagement in various classroom activities. Although well suited to the objectives of the evaluation, however, the approach used here can be fairly burdensome to implement and requires substantial commitment of resources. The evaluation team might have addressed the need for substantial investment of resources in several ways. They could have targeted a much smaller number of schools, thereby making it feasible for the disability area specialists to do the observations; the project then would have taken place over a longer period of time. Or they might have identified other, less critical personnel to do the observing in place of the counselors or specialists. For example, it might have been possible to use instructional aides. Finally, the team might have considered the possibility of doing fewer observations per classroom. It is possible that three or four observations would have been sufficient to provide an accurate assessment of students' in-class activities.

Possible Misinterpretations

Results from this evaluation could lead one to conclude that exceptional children in Lafayette County's elementary school programs are spending their special education class time in generally appropriate ways. Students seemed to spend the majority of their time actively engaged in academic tasks or academically related activities. A relatively small amount of off-task student behavior was seen. Although some instructional time was being lost to management concerns, this is an area where improvements can easily be made.

Several cautions, however, should be considered in interpreting these results. First, the observation system was not designed to provide highly specific information regarding the nature of the instructional tasks given students. Were these tasks linked to appropriate instructional goals for individual students? Did they reflect appropriate levels of difficulty? It may be the case that although students were engaged actively in academic and academically related tasks, the things they were working on did not match with their particular instructional needs. With this in mind, data provided by this evaluation should be considered as suggestive rather than conclusive.

It is also important to note that results for any evaluation involving observation will be influenced by the consistency and reliability of those doing the observations. Although the evaluation team in this example took steps to monitor observer reliability, changes in observer performance could have occurred over time, and thus results might reflect between-observer differences. If so, the validity of the reported observations might be subject to question.

Finally, it is important to keep clear the distinction between aggregate and individual data. Outcomes reported at the level of classrooms can be misleading when viewed in isolation. The aggregated pattern seen for a particular class may represent behavior that is fairly consistent across students, but it is also possible that undesirable behaviors may reflect almost exclusively the behavior of a small number of students. In order to address this concern, it is clear that some consideration should be given to analyzing outcomes at the level of individual students. Analysis of results for individual students might also provide a means of targeting intervention efforts most effectively.

5 Vignette Five

What's in an Individualized Educational Plan (IEP)?

Where, What, and Why

Washington High School was built in 1982 and serves students in grades 9-12; approximately 900 students are enrolled at Washington. This relatively new facility was built to accommodate an increase in enrollment realized as a result of a merger in which the Washington School District was combined with the Cherry Hills and Carbondale school districts to form the Washington Consolidated School System. The new system draws students from the city of Washington (population 175,000), as well as from several small towns and rural areas. The students who attend Washington are quite diverse in terms of their backgrounds.

When Washington first opened, Dr. Carolyn Spencer was appointed as its principal. She had taught in the old high school for 7 years and had also served as vice principal there for 3 years. She was seen as a good choice for principal of the new building because she already had established a positive working relationship with many of the school's teachers and was judged by them to be both fair and knowledgeable. It was felt these were especially critical characteristics for the new principal, because she would have to facilitate the smooth transition of faculty from several districts into a merged setting.

Dr. Spencer and her staff have accomplished much at Washington in the 8 years since the merger took place. They have established a positive tone within the school and a sense of pride in the programs offered there. The faculty seems committed to high-quality education and to the youngsters they serve. Moreover, the staff has worked together under Dr. Spencer's direction to improve the effectiveness of the school and its programs by designing and implementing a series of self-initiated program evaluation projects. The staff has been willing to participate in an ongoing program of evaluation activities because they know their efforts will not be in vain; results will be used to make positive changes in programs.

Focus on Special Education Programs

From the time the school first opened, evaluation has been used to study aspects of the school's mathematics and science programs, its counseling programs, its staff development programs, and its instructional support services. After consulting with her teachers, Dr. Spencer decided that the main focus of evaluation this year should be on the school's special education program. She knew that special education programming at the secondary level is a relatively recent trend in comparison to elementary-level programming and that it is not uncommon for such programs to be only marginally effective. Although she believed the program at Washington had quite a few strengths, Dr. Spencer also knew there was room for improvement based on feedback she had received from both regular and special class teachers.

Dr. Spencer discussed this proposed evaluation focus with the faculty at the first staff meeting of the school year. She made certain everyone knew that the special education teachers were not the target of the evaluation, but that the principal focus would be on the program itself. The faculty seemed to understand this and agreed that they would like to learn more about the program's strengths and weaknesses. The special education teachers were especially interested in the project; if they could do a better job, they wanted to know how.

After the faculty meeting, Dr. Spencer met separately with the school's six special education teachers to begin planning the evaluation project. The school's counselor, Ms. Valford, and the head of the vocational education program, Mr. Harkins, also attended, because they were involved in providing services to special students through their respective roles. It was decided that the head of the special education program, Ms. Engle, would lead the evaluation team, and all others who attended the meeting agreed to serve on the team. Dr. Spencer indicated that Carolyn Spooner, a research specialist from the district's central office, had agreed to assist the evaluation team as necessary. She would be able to provide expert guidance to help them along the way.

Focus for the Evaluation

The first meeting of the evaluation team was devoted to focusing their activities. The group knew it would be impractical to try to evaluate the whole special education program. There were far too many facets to the program, and too few evaluation resources were available. Instead, the team decided to identify a small number of areas that they considered to be of highest priority. They then would select one area from the list for their initial focus and address the others later in the year or during the following school year.

After much discussion, several issues emerged as priority concerns. These included an interest in assessing the training needed by both regular and special class teachers so that they could better address the education of students with special needs. Results from this evaluation were to aid in designing appropriate staff development activities for teachers. The evaluation team also felt it would be useful to evaluate the adequacy of instructional materials available to teach students, so that documentation could be provided to support requests for additional resources. In addition, the team felt it would be important to get a sense of the extent to which transition goals and objectives were being incorporated into IEPs (see Resource A, Indicator 11.1). They knew attention to transition concerns would influence significantly how well students were being prepared to leave school and to function on their own as productive members of society. The team felt that the extent to which this goal was being achieved would be related closely to the overall quality of the school's special education program.

As a result of continued discussion, the team members decided to focus their immediate evaluation on the transition goals and objectives issue.

Use of Transition Goals and Objectives in IEPs

How to Evaluate?

The next step was to consider the different ways in which the evaluation could be accomplished (see Chapter 3 of the general guide for further discussion). Ms. Valford suggested that one possible option would be for her, together with Mr. Harkins and Dr. Spencer, to develop a short questionnaire or survey to which the six special education teachers could respond. Items on the questionnaire or survey would specify common transition goals and objectives. Respondents would be asked to indicate the extent to which they felt these transition objectives were included explicitly in the IEPs they developed for their students. This idea was rejected following some discussion, because it was felt that teachers would be responding on the basis of their global perceptions of what they included and that they might not reflect accurately what was actually in individual IEPs. As an alternative, it was suggested that the team develop a procedure for reviewing teachers' lesson plans. The members felt this would not only show which transition goals were being addressed in instruction but also provide information on the amount of time being devoted to various transition concerns. But the team members decided to rule out this option as well, at least for the time being, when they realized how difficult it might be to determine whether some of the notations in a teacher's plan book were linked directly to specific transition objectives. The team felt this approach would be a viable option only if it was paired with teacher interviews, a method that everyone felt would be too time-consuming.

It finally was agreed that a suitable data collection strategy would be to review IEPs directly, using some form of checklist as a guide. The team members felt this method would provide them with important preliminary information and that it would not require extensive time commitments on the part of evaluators or those providing the information. Information gained through the team's reviews would indicate the extent to which transition objectives were intended to be a part of the curriculum for special needs students. If, in fact, such objectives were being included in IEPs, subsequent evaluations of teachers' plan books (coupled with teacher interviews) could be conducted to determine how well these goals were being addressed in classrooms. If such goals were not included routinely in IEPs, it would follow that one would not expect to see them included in instructional plans; therefore, there would be no need to examine the issue further.

Identification of Essential Transition Objectives

Once the evaluation team members decided on their approach, they were ready to work out a specific plan. It was agreed that, prior to their next meeting, everyone would try to identify some of the essential transition objectives likely to be needed by exceptional students at the secondary level. These were to be derived from professional literature or based on experience. Ms. Engle volunteered to review materials available from the central office that were related to program evaluation and to assemble pertinent information to assist the team in planning. She was interested particularly in learning how to determine the number of IEPs the team should review.

Ms. Engle began the next meeting by proposing a plan for selecting a sample of IEPs that she had developed as a result of her reading. She indicated that they would not have to review every IEP in order to draw valid conclusions. Her plan reflected the fact that the special education program served 168 students and that each of the program's six teachers developed IEPs for 28 of these students. She proposed that each teacher give Dr. Spencer an anonymous roster that listed the names of students for whom the teacher prepared IEPs, a total of six rosters in all. Dr. Spencer, in turn, would distribute these to

Ms. Engle, Ms. Valford, and Mr. Harkins so that each of them received two rosters. In the event that Ms. Engle received a copy of her own student list, she would return it to Dr. Spencer, who would replace it with another list. These three team members would be responsible for completing the review of IEP documents, none of which had been written by them for their own students, thereby limiting potential reviewer bias. Others on the team (i.e., the five remaining special education teachers) would be involved in other activities, such as preparing checklist materials and summarizing outcomes. By distributing responsibilities in this fashion, Ms. Engle hoped to minimize the burden imposed on each participant.

The individuals reviewing IEPs were to locate the IEP file for every third student on their rosters as a means of selecting a sample for the evaluation. Because each roster contained approximately 28 names, this would result in a sample of 9 names per list, or a total of 54 IEP files from all six rosters. This represented a sampling of 32% of the total pool of 168 IEPs and meant that each of the three reviewers would have to review only 18 IEP documents. Ms. Engle indicated that on the basis of her reading, this sample would be of sufficient size to support acceptably precise conclusions.

Checklist

Next, the team members turned their attention to developing a checklist to guide review of the IEPs. As they shared their lists of important transition objectives, two things became apparent. There was reasonable agreement across lists as to the broad areas appropriate to a secondary-level transition curriculum. The areas identified by the team included aspects of social skill development, academic support skills, vocational skills, career awareness, and independent living/self-management skills. It was also quite clear that a wide variety of specific objectives could fit under each of these categories. With this in mind, it was decided that the checklist should be kept broad. Rather than attempting to include extensive lists of objectives to guide reviewers, the team members felt it would be better to use more general categories. They felt that although students would vary considerably with respect to their specific transition needs (i.e., the specific instructional objectives that were appropriate for them), the team was safe in assuming that some attention to one or more of the broad transition curriculum categories would be appropriate for all students.

Developing a Checklist

On the basis of this discussion, the special education teachers developed the checklist presented in Figure 5.1. In the left-hand column the team listed 12 broad categories widely held to be appropriate components of a transition curriculum. They also included an item called "Other" to give reviewers space to list objectives that seemed to be related to transition concerns but did not fit under any of the listed categories. On the right side of the page, the team provided space for reviewers to mark the frequency with which objectives related to each transition area were stated explicitly in the IEP. They provided space at the top of the form for reviewers to insert a small amount of descriptive information, such as the student's grade and his or her category of exceptionality. The team felt that this information might be helpful in analyzing the results.

The team also decided that it would be helpful for the reviewers to practice using the checklist prior to collecting data. The members felt this would give reviewers a chance to clarify what was meant by each of the listed transition areas and to practice identifying the specific objectives that were subsumed under each broad category. It was agreed that each data collector would review the same set of six IEPs pulled from the files of students who had graduated. This would allow them to make certain that they were consistent in selecting the categories under which specific objectives would fit.

Results

The review of IEPs was completed 4 weeks after the evaluation team's initial meeting. The checklists were then given to the five team members who had been designated to summarize the findings. Three team members were responsible for completing a frequency summary of the results; this was done using a blank copy of the checklist. They indicated in the frequency column the number of times reviewers had located explicitly stated goals that could be categorized within the broad transition areas listed on the checklist. For example, their summary of outcomes related to Goals 1 and 2 looked like this:

Transition Area	*Frequency of Occurrence*
Social Skill and Affective Development	
1. General social skills	/ / / /
2. School-related social skills	/ / / / /

These results indicate that in only four instances did reviewers find goals related to development of general social skills explicitly stated in the IEP files sampled. Goals concerned with development of school-related social skills were located only five times.

When results from all of the checklists had been summarized on the composite form, team members found they had recorded a total of 168 entries across the categories shown on the checklist. Before moving on, however, they carefully rechecked their work to verify the accuracy of their findings. Next, two team members who were not

Transition Goal Checklist

Student Grade: _____

Type Placement: _____

Reviewer: _____

Transition Area   *Frequency of Occurrence*

Social Skills and Affective Development
1. General social skills _____
2. School-related social skills _____
3. Employment-related social skills _____

Academic Support Skills
4. Study skills _____
5. Learning strategies _____

Vocational Skill Development
6. General vocational skills _____
7. Specific vocational preparation _____

Career Awareness
8. Understanding occupational roles and alternatives _____

Independent Living/Self-Management Skills
9. Leisure skills _____
10. Home and family skills _____
11. Understanding health concerns _____
12. Community living skills _____

Other
13. _____ _____

Figure 5.1. Transition Goal Checklist

involved in summarizing data related to the frequency of goal occurrence were responsible for converting the response counts into percentages. They did so by dividing the number of responses recorded for each transition-goal category count by the total number of transition goals recorded across the 54 IEPs sampled (i.e., 186). Figure 5.2 presents the results that were obtained when the checklist responses were analyzed in this fashion.

Transition Goal Checklist	
Student Grade: _____	
Type Placement: _____	
Reviewer: _____	

Transition Area	*Frequency of Occurrence*
Social Skills and Affective Development	
1. General social skills	//// (2%)
2. School-related social skills	///// (3%)
3. Employment-related social skills	/// (1%)
Academic Support Skills	
4. Study skills	///// ///// ///// ///// // (12%)
5. Learning strategies	///// ///// ///// // (9%)
Vocational Skill Development	
6. General vocational skills	///// ///// ///// ///// ///// / (14%)
7. Specific vocational preparation	///// ///// ///// // (9%)
Career Awareness	
8. Understanding occupational roles and alternatives	///// ///// ///// ///// / (11%)
Independent Living/Self-Management Skills	
9. Leisure skills	// (1%)
10. Home and family skills	///// ///// / (6%)
11. Understanding health concerns	///// ///// ///// ///// ///// ///// ///// / (19%)
12. Community living skills	///// / (3%)
Other	
13. Applying to college	///// ///// (5%)
14. Self-advocacy	///// / (3%)

Figure 5.2. Summary of Results Related to Frequency Counts

Summarizing the Results

In addition to summarizing the results in the manner shown in Figure 5.2, the two team members who were responsible for calculating the percentages prepared a second type of data summary. They were interested in determining the number of transition objectives typically included in IEPs regardless of their category type. They knew that the number of objectives appropriate for a given student would be dependent on that student's particular needs; therefore, they could not specify an exact number of goals that should be included

# of objectives	# of objectives
0. _/ / /_ (5%)	6. _0_
1. _/////_ (9%)	7. _0_
2. _///// ///// ///// ///// //_ (41%)	8. _0_
3. _///// ///// ///// //_ (31%)	9. _0_
4. _///// //_ (13%)	10. _0_
5. _0_ (0%)	11. _0_

Figure 5.3. Frequency of Transition Objectives in IEPs

for an IEP to be judged as adequate with respect to inclusion of transition objectives. They felt safe in assuming, however, that a minimum of at least two transition objectives would be appropriate for all secondary-level special education students. Their analysis was designed to show the extent to which this was the case. The team members completed their analysis by totaling the number of objectives listed on each of the completed checklists and tallying that number on a summary form as shown in Figure 5.3.

Interpretation

Results of the analyses concerned with the extent to which transition goals were being included in students' IEPs were quite encouraging to the evaluation team. As shown in Figure 5.3, two IEP objectives were included in 41% of the IEP documents sampled. An additional 28% of the IEPs had three transition objectives specified, and 13% of the sample included four such objectives. Taken as a whole, the team found that 85% of the IEPs sampled contained at least two transition objectives. Most important, they found that only 14% of the IEPs contained fewer than two transition objectives, thereby falling below the level of acceptability established by the team prior to analyzing the data (i.e., to be considered adequate, IEPs had to include a minimum of two transition objectives). These results were interpreted to mean that the special education program was doing a reasonably good job of meeting the goal of incorporating transition objectives and plans into IEPs for students at the secondary level.

Analysis of results related to the types of transition goals included in the IEPs also proved to be quite interesting. From the information provided in Figure 5.2, it can be seen that certain transition areas seemed to be addressed far more frequently than others. For example, it appears that transition objectives were most likely to deal with academic support skills, vocational skill development, and/or career awareness. Objectives dealing with independent living and self-management skills appeared far less frequently, with the exception of those related to understanding health concerns (perhaps this is because students typically are required to take a health course in conjunction with their physical education class). Objectives related to various aspects of social skill development rarely were included in the IEPs, a finding that was quite surprising given the frequency with which handicapped adolescents are described as having significant social skill deficits. The results also showed that in addition to addressing the transition areas listed on the checklist in varying degrees, the special education teachers placed some emphasis on teaching students how to apply to college programs and how to serve as advocates for themselves.

Use of Results

Once the results were available, Dr. Spencer held a meeting of the evaluation team to discuss the study's findings and to develop a plan for making use of the findings. It was decided that although the special education teachers seemed to be doing a good job of including transition objectives in students' IEPs, there might be some room for improvement. Everyone agreed to monitor more closely instances where they were developing IEPs that did not include transition goals or included only one such goal. The idea was to make certain that limited use of transition goals occurred only in instances when it was warranted in light of a student's particular needs. The team also decided that their failure to place greater emphasis on social skill development and development of independent living/self-management skills was probably more reflective of their own lack of knowledge than a limited need for such skills among their students. It was agreed that Ms. Engle would work with Dr. Spencer to identify curriculum materials and/or staff development options that would address this concern. Finally, it was decided, in keeping with the school's ongoing commitment to program evaluation, that it would be important to share the results of this project, as well as plans developed to address program weaknesses, with the faculty as a whole.

Summary of Evaluation Principles

This example illustrated several important principles that should be kept in mind in implementing an evaluation of special education programs such as the one described here. As in other examples included in this guide, we have provided a list of these principles below:

1. Do not attempt to evaluate every aspect of the program at once. Focus the evaluation by limiting your efforts to a few priority concerns.
2. When choosing a method of data collection, try to select a strategy that minimizes the burden on those who will provide information and that can be implemented in light of your resources.
3. If at all possible, design the evaluation in ways that permit those who provide information to preserve their privacy. Always guarantee confidentiality; if possible, provide anonymity.
4. Establish criteria for interpreting the outcomes beforehand. In the present example, the evaluation team decided that IEPs should include a minimum of two transition objectives in order to be considered adequate.
5. If a checklist is used, data collectors should be given ample opportunity to practice using it prior to collecting actual data. Training should include opportunities to clarify terms and descriptors used in the checklist.
6. It is useful to have data collectors practice using a checklist by collecting data on the same events, activities, or products to be observed during the observation. This allows you to determine the extent to which their judgments are consistent. In order to draw valid conclusions, you should have at least 90% agreement among data collectors; disagreements should be resolved through discussion.
7. If a checklist will be used in conjunction with a product review, as in this example, it is essential that the number of products reviewed be large enough to provide an adequate reflection of the characteristic you intend to measure (e.g., the extent to which transition objectives are included in IEPs).

Alternatives to the Strategy Used Here

As stated earlier, the evaluation team considered a number of alternatives for collecting information on the extent to which transition objectives were being included in IEPs, including the possibility of teacher interviews and a review of teachers' planning books. Although both of these options were rejected initially, the evaluation team might have gained some additional insights by using these data collection strategies in combination after they had completed their review of student IEPs. This approach would allow the team to assess the extent to which transition objectives actually were being addressed in practice. Although the checklist results suggested that special education teachers at Washington were doing a reasonably good job of including transition objectives in their IEPs, it may be the case that teachers are not addressing these goals through their instruction. By collecting additional data through teacher interviews and reviews of planning books, the evaluation team might get a better sense of the incorporation of transition goals and objectives in the special education program. Information obtained from the checklist data collection strategy would be enormously helpful in guiding the development of interviews and plan-book review procedures.

Possible Misinterpretations

There are two cautions that should be kept in mind in interpreting the results of this program evaluation. As pointed out earlier, use of the checklist provided little information on the extent to which teachers actually were implementing programs to address the transition objectives specified in their IEPs. The adequacy of the program's transition efforts is being inferred from the checklist results; the actual program students receive may be considerably less extensive than the results suggest. Also, no attempt was made to examine the extent to which the transition goals and objectives listed for particular students were appropriate for their needs. It could be that the nature and/or number of objectives listed for students was insufficient.

6
Vignette Six

Assessing the Generalization of Skills to Other Settings

Where, What, and Why

Chandler Hills Developmental Learning Center enrolls 145 special students who reside in or around the suburban town of Stratton. Thirty miles from a major urban area, Stratton offers an attractive housing alternative for professionals and others who commute to work in the city and choose to live in suburbia. Although all economic levels are represented in the community, Stratton's residents are typically white-collar professionals. The racial mix is 70% white, 26% black, and 4% other ethnic groups.

Regular Education Initiative

Chandler Hills is recognized widely as having a model program for children with disabilities. Students are transported from miles around to this facility, which for 22 years has provided excellent programs for children with all types and degrees of handicapping conditions. The regular education initiative (REI) of the past decade, with its accompanying concern for integrated service delivery, has resulted in some changes in the student population of Chandler Hills. Some classes now are mainstreamed into public school buildings, and some of the higher-functioning children are mainstreamed into classrooms with normally developing children. Certain classifications of exceptional children, however, appropriately are still served at Chandler Hills. These groups include some children who are classified as severely/profoundly mentally handicapped (S/PMH).

Anna Goodson, teacher of the S/PMH class, devoted a portion of the past summer to developing new intervention strategies for her students, with a primary focus on self-help skills. Although she always had viewed her current curriculum guide as adequate, she was not convinced that it contained all she needed to make significant improvements in her program. After reading several informative articles in professional journals, Ms. Goodson realized that although her program goals were surprisingly similar to those found in the literature, the assessment component of her curriculum was less than adequate, especially with regard to assessing the generalization of target skills for students to settings other than her classroom. Ms. Goodson expressed her views to her director, J. B. Carr, who shared her concerns and told her that he was forming a committee to evaluate the entire testing program at Chandler Hills. He invited Ms. Goodson to serve on the committee, and she accepted. He explained to her that he and other area program directors had met to discuss mutual concerns and had located an excellent resource for program evaluation. He gave her a copy of *Special Education Programs: A Guide to Evaluation* and the accompanying general guide from the Essential Tools for Educators series and informed her that the committee was scheduled to begin work during the week prior to the opening of the new school year.

Focus for the Evaluation

Generalization of Skills

As Ms. Goodson began working with the committee to evaluate the testing program at Chandler Hills, she recognized that her own immediate needs were much narrower than those of the committee. She was interested specifically in knowing whether her students were using skills at home that they had learned at school. Because she was planning to implement her new program of self-help intervention strategies at the beginning of the school year, she felt she needed almost immediate access to an instrument that would help her obtain information concerning how well her students' newly acquired skills generalized to their home settings. When it became clear that the committee's task was quite large and would extend over the entire school year, if not beyond, Ms. Goodson decided to create her own data collection instrument and to use it during the coming year. She had noted that among the standards and indicators of quality of special education programs listed in the *Special Education Programs: A Guide to Evaluation,* Indicator 12.2 ("Assessment includes consideration of places and settings beyond the school classroom where the S/PMH student functions") addressed her specific concerns precisely. Ms. Goodson reasoned that other members of the testing committee might be willing to support her efforts to design a data collection instrument, especially if it was related directly to one of the standards from the program evaluation guide. She felt they might view development of her instrument as a point of departure for at least a part of their broader task of program evaluation at Chandler Hills.

Measurement Instrument

Ms. Goodson wanted to construct an instrument that would help her determine whether certain skills addressed at school were being practiced at home by her students. She began reading the books from the ETE series and quickly realized they would be an invaluable resource for her. She found the section about collecting information in Chapter 3 of the general guide and read with interest about possible sources of information. She decided the most appropriate source of the information she desired would be the parents of her students. She read further in Chapter 3 of the general guide and learned about common formal methods and instruments used to gather data from parents. Consulting the special education program guide, she found that the data collection strategies listed for Indicator 12.2 were checklist, survey, and questionnaire. Checking back in the general guide, she read that surveys normally were conducted with a large number of respondents. She decided against using a survey, because she needed information from only six people.

Use of Naturalistic Observation Procedures

Considering the relative merits of a questionnaire and a checklist, Ms. Goodson opted for a checklist, because it seemed to her that the information she desired was very specific, easy to list, and would lend itself well to a simple observation checklist. She wanted to keep her instrument simple in order to reduce the burden on parents as much as possible. Noting in the general guide's discussion of unobtrusive measures the importance of gathering information in ways that do not affect the natural behavior of those being observed, Ms. Goodson felt that data concerning students' behaviors at home would probably be recorded most effectively by a parent or someone who routinely spent large blocks of time in the student's home environment.

As Ms. Goodson began the actual construction of her observation checklist, she recalled reading in the general guide that observation checklists are often best selected from existing instruments rather than generated from scratch. Using the resources provided in the ETE series and a few checklists encountered earlier in professional journals, Ms. Goodson found several that were related to her needs. None of them, however, contained the exact skills she had targeted in her intervention program. In checking her S/PMH curriculum guide, from which she had selected several target skills, Ms. Goodson again found checklists, but none that met her needs. Ms. Goodson concluded that the existing instruments she had found would help her by providing suggested formats, but she would need to generate her own specific content. Because it was important that she link her assessment to the specific intervention strategies used in her classroom, Ms. Goodson prepared a list of target skills. She then checked this list against her curriculum guide to make sure it reflected her instructional objectives as closely as possible. Finally, Ms. Goodson categorized her list into three broad headings: washing, grooming, and feeding.

When Ms. Goodson began to consider how to format her observation checklist, she noted that some sample checklists used columns for documenting the degree to which skills have been mastered. She understood that certain behaviors require assistance for a period of time before mastery is exhibited at the independent level. Feeling that this format was appropriate for her S/PMH students, Ms. Goodson decided to provide three columns for respondents, designated as follows: (a) I do this for my child; (b) my child can do this with help; and (c) my child does this without assistance. She created a rough draft, listing the target skills in their respective categories on the left, and provided three columns in which responses could be recorded.

At this point, Ms. Goodson decided to share her working draft of the observation checklist with members of the program evaluation committee at Chandler Hills to solicit their comments. Dr. James Patrick, professor of special education from a local university, was noted for his expertise in program evaluation and had agreed to serve as a special consultant to the committee. He complimented Ms. Goodson's efforts at program improvement and suggested that collecting data on the behaviors of her students would help her to evaluate the effectiveness of her intervention strategies. The data would enable her to identify which students had and had not accomplished the goals of a particular intervention. Data then could be summarized to help determine the overall effectiveness of the program. Dr. Patrick suggested that Ms. Goodson might consider administering her checklist at the beginning of the school year, at some point around midyear, and then again at the end of the year. He pointed out that ongoing, or formative, evaluation could yield valuable information that would be useful in refining her program and her evaluation instrument. The committee concurred. Ms. Goodson therefore decided to administer her observation checklist in September, January, and May. This would enable her to use the checklist to document the progression of students' skills acquisition over time. Ms. Goodson's observation checklist is represented in Figure 6.1.

Student _____   Parent _____
Date of Observation _____

Please place letter A, B, or C beside each item using the following code: A = I do this for my child; B = my child does this with assistance; C = my child does this without assistance.

Washing:
   1. Dries hands   _____
   2. Washes hands without soap   _____
   3. Washes hands with soap   _____
   4. Washes face   _____
   5. Dries face   _____
   6. Knows which faucet is hot and which is cold   _____
   7. Turns faucet off and on   _____
   8. Adjusts water temperature   _____

Grooming:
   9. Wipes nose with reminder   _____
  10. Wipes nose without reminder   _____
  11. Combs/brushes hair   _____
  12. Brushes teeth   _____

Feeding:
  13. Feeds self finger foods   _____
  14. Feeds self with spoon   _____
  15. Uses fork appropriately   _____
  16. Uses napkin to wipe mouth   _____
  17. Discards trash when finished eating   _____

Figure 6.1. Self-Help Skills Observation Checklist (Blank)

Field-Testing the Instrument

At the next meeting of the program evaluation committee, Ms. Goodson shared her observation checklist with committee members. Mrs. Brittain, a teacher of orthopedically impaired students, suggested that the checklist probably should be field-tested to see if there were any kinks that needed to be worked out. Two of her students were severely mentally handicapped in addition to being orthopedically involved. Mrs. Brittain was confident the parents of these two students would be willing to complete the checklist based on observation of their own children, thereby providing an appropriate, albeit small, sample with which to field-test the instrument. Ms. Goodson called the parents of the two children and found that they, indeed, were willing to cooperate. She arranged a meeting to describe her program and to explain her need for their assistance. They took copies of the observation checklist home and promised to return the completed checklist, with comments, within a week. Feedback from the two parents was generally positive; however, both mentioned problems with items 9 and 10. The phrases *with reminder* and *without reminder* were confusing as they tried to decide on the degree of independence the child exhibited. Reminders were interpreted as a form of assistance, thereby confusing the parents as they attempted to respond to these items. As a result, Ms. Goodson decided that the two items should be collapsed into one, deleting any reference to verbal reminders. The only other problem area expressed during field-testing was the issue of whether all the target skills represented on the checklist were indeed realistic for S/PMH students. One of the students involved in the field test was impaired orthopedically to the extent that certain skills (e.g., combs/brushes hair or brushes teeth without assistance) were considered unrealistic expectations for him. Ms. Goodson discussed this issue with other committee members and decided that although each child would not necessarily achieve each goal at the independent level, the checklist should still reflect the self-help skills that were included in her intervention program. She individualized her expectations within the classroom and discussed with parents on a regular basis the need for realistic expectations at home. She concluded that the design of the checklist itself resolved the issue, in that the first column ("I do this for my child") would in some cases be the only realistic response for certain students.

Administration of the Checklist

As. Dr. Patrick had suggested, Ms. Goodson decided to use the checklist as an informal pre- and postintervention observation device. When she visited the homes of her students during the first week of the school year, she discussed with each parent her goals for the child and her new program targeting self-help skills. She solicited parents' views concerning their priorities for self-help goals, and together they determined appropriate target skills for the child. She also discussed degrees of skill independence appropriate for their child and asked that parents help her decide, for each skill, the extent to which total independence would be a realistic expectation for the child. When agreement had been reached, Ms. Goodson showed parents her observation checklist. Because the validity of information gained from the checklist would depend to a large degree on the consistency with which respondents defined the behaviors being observed, Ms. Goodson discussed each item in detail until she was sure that she and the parents were in agreement as to how each target skill was defined. When she was confident they were in agreement, Ms. Goodson asked the parents to complete the observation checklist at that time, based on their observations of their child as they recalled them at that point. She asked the parents to remain objective as observers, reminding them that the skills represented goals for their child and that they should not interpret any of their responses as indicating failure on anyone's part. Ms. Goodson waited for the parents to complete the checklist so that she could answer any questions that might arise. At the conclusion of the visit, Ms. Goodson thanked the parents for their cooperation and reminded them that parent involvement was critical to the success of any program of intervention with handicapped children.

Obtaining Information at Parent Conferences

Midyear parent conferences were held in January, at which time Ms. Goodson gave each parent a new copy of the checklist they had completed at the beginning of the year. Because they were now familiar with the instrument, she left it with them, requesting that they return it to her within a week. Within the week, Ms. Goodson received four of the six checklists. She made phone calls to remind the two parents who had not responded that she needed the information as soon as possible. She received one the following day. The sixth checklist was not received until two weeks later because the envelope had been addressed incorrectly and returned to the parents' home; the parents had been out of town for several days and had not realized their error until their return. This served to remind Ms. Goodson that self-addressed stamped return envelopes will usually expedite the return of important documents from home to school.

Finally, in May, when IEP conferences were held, parents completed the checklist a third time. Learning from her midyear experience with delays, Ms. Goodson provided a self-addressed stamped envelope with each checklist in order to facilitate the prompt return of completed observation checklists. All six checklists were received within a few days.

Results and Interpretation

After the first administration of the checklist in September, Ms. Goodson calculated the percentages of level A, B, and C responses for each student. Her objective in summarizing the checklist data at this point was to obtain baseline data on percentages of target skills currently performed by or for each child. Ms. Goodson found that she needed to add spaces at the end of the checklist in which she could record percentages for each observation. Figure 6.2 shows the checklist as completed by Mary's mother during the first observation period, with percentages added by Ms. Goodson.

Upon examining the results of the first administration of her observation checklist in September, Ms. Goodson noted that most of the

Student ___Mary___ Parent _____

Date of Observation _____

Please place letter A, B, or C beside each item, using the following code:
A = I do this for my child, B = My child does this with assistance, C = My child does this without assistance.

Washing:

  1. Dries hands — B
  2. Washes hands without soap — B
  3. Washes hands with soap — A
  4. Washes face — A
  5. Dries face — A
  6. Knows which faucet is hot and which is cold — A
  7. Turns faucet off and on — A
  8. Adjusts water temperature — A

Grooming:

  9. Wipes nose — A
  10. Combs/brushes hair — A
  11. Brushes teeth — A

Feeding:

  12. Feeds self finger foods — C
  13. Feeds self with spoon — B
  14. Uses fork appropriately — A
  15. Uses napkin to wipe mouth — A
  16. Discards trash when finished eating — A

I do this for my child	% A	75%
My child does this with assistance	% B	19%
My child does this without assistance	% C	6%

Please use the following space to comment on any observations you wish to share:

Figure 6.2. Mary's Self-Help Skills Observation Checklist

targeted self-help skills were being performed for the children by their parents at home. For example, she found in September that Mary's mother was performing 75% (12 to 16 items) of the tasks for her and providing assistance on an additional 19% (3 of 16 items). Mary was exhibiting independence on only 6% (1 of 16 items) of the targeted self-help skills observed at the beginning of the year. Likewise with her other students, Ms. Goodson noticed that none of her students was observed performing more than 3 of the 16 skills independently. Across her six students, the range for the third column (independence) was 6% to 19%, whereas the range for the first column (done for child) was 56% to 75%. This was not surprising; in fact, it confirmed for Ms. Goodson the appropriateness of her efforts to revise her self-help skills intervention program.

Summarizing the Results

In addition to documenting individual progress for each of her students throughout the year, Ms. Goodson was also interested in seeing the progress of the group as a whole. She reasoned that analyzing group progress would help her to determine how well her interventions were working. Ms. Goodson designed a summary sheet that would demonstrate group progress as well as individual gains. She transferred percentages for levels A, B, and C from each individual checklist onto her summary sheet and then included a number in parentheses to represent the number of checklist items in that category. Table 6.1 shows Ms. Goodson's data summary at the end of the first observation.

Subsequent checklists in January and in May indicated that generalization was indeed occurring. As Ms. Goodson entered new data on her summary sheet in January, she noticed that each of her six students had made gains in the number of skills they were performing independently (ranging from 6 to 12 points) and on the number of skills they were performing with assistance (ranging from 6 to 24 points). As a result, there were noticeable reductions (ranging from 13 to 25 points) in the percentages of checklist items performed for children by a parent. Likewise in May, the gains in independence were noticeable for each child. Table 6.2 shows Ms. Goodson's summary sheet as completed after the third observation at the end of the school year. She had expanded the summary sheet to include space for recording group averages as well as individual gains.

Use of Results

As Ms. Goodson analyzed the data she had collected and recorded on her summary sheet, she was pleased to note that there had been an important reduction in the percentage of target skills performed for her students at home. The reductions per child ranged from 37 to 57 percentage points, with an overall group average reduction of 42 percentage points. At the same time, there was an important increase in the percentage of skills performed independently by the students at home. Percentage increases ranged from 25 to 31 points, with an overall group average gain of 28 percentage points. Ms. Goodson interpreted these results as indicating that her intervention program had been a successful one.

TABLE 6.1 Self-Help Skills Summary (First Observation)

	Percentage Each Category per Evaluation								
	September			*January*			*May*		
	A	B	C	A	B	C	A	B	C
Mary	75% (19)	19% (3)	06% (1)						
Joyce	69% (11)	19% (3)	12% (2)						
David	56% (9)	25% (4)	19% (3)						
Desmond	63% (10)	25% (4)	12% (2)						
Paula	63% (10)	31% (5)	06% (1)						
Charles	69% (11)	12% (2)	19% (3)						

LEGEND: A: done for child; B: child does with help; C: child does for self

TABLE 6.2 Self-Help Skills Summary (Completed)

Percentage Each Category Per Evaluation Plus Short-Term and Long-Term Reductions/Gains

	September			January						May						Overall Reductions/Gains in Percentage Points From September to May per Child		
	A	B	C	A		B		C		A		B		C		A	B	C
Mary	75% (12)	19% (3)	6% (1)	50% (8) −25		38% (6) +19		12% (2) +6		38% (6) −12		31% (5) −7		31% (5) +19		−37	+12	+25
Joyce	69% (11)	19% (3)	12% (2)	38% (6) −21		43% (7) +24		19% (3) +7		25% (4) −13		38% (6) −5		38% (6) +19		−44	+19	+26
David	56% (9)	25% (4)	19% (3)	31% (5) −25		38% (6) +15		31% (5) +12		19% (3) −12		31% (5) −7		50% (8) +19		−37	+6	+31
Desmond	63% (10)	25% (4)	12% (2)	50% (8) −13		31% (5) +6		19% (3) +7		25% (4) −25		31% (5) —		44% (7) +25		−38	+6	+32
Paula	63% (10)	31% (5)	6% (1)	44% (7) −19		44% (7) +13		12% (20) +6		25% (4) −19		44% (7) —		31% (5) +19		−38	+13	+25
Charles	69% (11)	12% (2)	19% (3)	50% (8) −19		25% (4) +13		25% (4) +6		12% (2) −38		38% (6) +13		50% (8) +25		−57	+26	31
									Average reduction/gain in percentage points for group						−42	+14	+28

LEGEND: A: done for child; B: child does with help; C: child does for self.

Attempting to analyze the second column (gains in percentage of target skills performed with assistance), Ms. Goodson recognized that it would be difficult to draw conclusions for the group from this column because items moving to the third column (independence) were being replaced with items from the first column (done for child). She decided that closer examination of all data in the second column, with reference to the original checklists, would be necessary to her analysis of individual gains. Looking at the numbers in parentheses on her summary sheet (number of checklist items represented in that category), Ms. Goodson referred to the original checklist to determine which items fell into the second column. She noted for each child which skills generalized quickly (i.e, moved from the first column to the third) and which skills had not generalized (i.e., either moved from the first column to the second or did not move). Ms. Goodson carefully checked the skills remaining in the first column and compared them to the individual students' IEPs, verifying whether these were skills that had been judged at the beginning of the year to be appropriate for the child in question. Ms. Goodson then made notes concerning the target skills remaining in the second column so that she could discuss her continuing efforts with parents at the start of the next year. In her final report to parents, Ms. Goodson included a copy of each child's observation checklist and reminded parents of the benefit of continued practice in order to maintain the skills students had learned and to generalize further those being learned.

Summary of Evaluation Principles

1. Do not attempt to evaluate every aspect of a program at once. Focus the evaluation by selecting one or two indicators of quality from Resource A.
2. When choosing a method of data collection, try to select an alternative that minimizes the burden on those who will be asked to provide the information.
3. Whenever possible, choose unobtrusive measures so that the natural behaviors of those being studied are not affected.
4. Make sure behaviors being observed are defined and understood clearly by everyone involved in the evaluation.
5. Checklist behaviors should be written as goals, not failures. Focus on what is to be achieved, not on behaviors the subject cannot demonstrate.

Alternatives to the Strategy Used Here

Several alternative methods of data collection could have been used in the current example. A survey, a collection of questions on a small number of issues given to a large number of potential respondents, would have been a possible choice and would have been especially appropriate had the number of parents been large. A questionnaire is a collection of standard questions about a few issues placed on a form for response, often locally developed because of the idiosyncratic nature of many issues. The use of a parent questionnaire would be a good choice if Ms. Goodson later chooses to involve parents in an evaluation of her intervention program. Telephone interviews offer another alternative and could be completed over a short period of time. This alternative would also eliminate the problem encountered with delays in return by mail. Ms. Goodson preferred to complete her data collection at the same time she met with parents to discuss mutual goals. Finally, Ms. Goodson might have used one of many existing observation checklists. This would have saved her considerable time. Because she was experimenting with new and very specific intervention techniques, however, she chose to design her own checklist to parallel the list of skills she had targeted for instruction.

Possible Misinterpretations

As with any measurement strategy, behaviors to be observed should be well-defined and understood by all involved. The extent to which the information obtained is valid will depend to a large degree on the consistency with which those who are observing subjects define the behaviors. Criteria for the accomplishment of tasks such as those in this example can vary considerably from parent to parent. It is extremely important that the parents who are observing and recording are defining the tasks in the same way as the teacher who is analyzing the data. It is also important to consider parents' objectivity when evaluating the results of an observation checklist such as this. The evaluator must be alert to any signs of bias that would compromise the validity of the instrument.

Critical to the interpretation of results illustrated in this example is the fact that it cannot be assumed that the observed results are based solely on the intervention. The effects of parent involvement can be significant, especially with special needs children. Parental effects and the effects of interactions with others (e.g., day care providers, other adults) must be considered in any evaluation of intervention programs.

Conclusion

This guide to the evaluation of special education programs reflects a strong belief that school personnel can do much to improve the quality of the instructional programs and service delivery options in their schools. They can do this by systematically evaluating programmatic quality using criteria found to be associated with effective special education programs. This guide was written to encourage school personnel (e.g., special educators, administrators, and school counselors) to think of evaluation as being more than an externally mandated activity to which they must respond. Illustrated in this guide are examples of school personnel initiating evaluations to meet their own program evaluation concerns. Each vignette was developed in a comprehensive manner to serve as a guide for others who may wish to carry out similar activities in their own settings. The vignettes are intended to provide insight into the evaluation process by showing in detail how one might implement the strategies and principles described in the general guide of this series when evaluating a special education program. We cannot emphasize enough the need for program evaluation in special education that goes beyond the question of legal compliance. It is no longer enough to know only that your programs are meeting federal mandates. Questions such as whether one is meeting program needs, whether specific elements in your programs need improvement, or whether programs are meeting their intended goals also need to be answered.

Resource A: Standards and Indicators for Evaluation of Special Education Programs With Suggested Evaluation Methods

This resource contains a set of standards and indicators of quality that can be used by a wide range of professionals who wish to evaluate their special education programs internally with the objective of securing information that will guide the improvement of these programs. With this purpose in mind, it was assumed that evaluation data most likely would be collected at the school level by school personnel and that the personnel involved in the evaluation would be doing so in addition to carrying out their routine responsibilities. As a result, standards and/or indicators that could not be measured precisely and adequately without excessive time commitments were not included in the list that follows. Indicators of programmatic quality suggested in the literature but lacking sufficient empirical support also were excluded.

The standards and indicators of quality listed in this resource were derived from comprehensive reviews of several complementary literatures on the characteristics of school-based special education programs. These reviews were concerned with the design, implementation, and assessment of special education programs and included a computerized literature search (ERIC). Sources identified in the professional literature also were augmented by a review of the educational evaluation practices of various states and of professional papers presented at recent meetings of the American Educational Research Association and the National Council on Measurement in Education.

Standard 1

Quality special education programs actively provide the staff resources necessary for program success.

1.1 Sufficient numbers of special and regular class teachers and related service personnel are employed to maintain effective teacher-student ratios.
Data source: Principal/special education teachers/annual program reports
Data collection strategy: Questionnaire/survey/checklist

1.2 Sufficient numbers of instructional aids are available to assist exceptional children in both special and mainstream classrooms.
Data source: Principal/special education teachers/annual program reports
Data collection strategy: Questionnaire/survey/checklist

1.3 Teachers, administrators, diagnostic personnel, and related service personnel are routinely available to carry out their full range of responsibilities relative to meeting the needs of exceptional children.
Data source: Special education teachers/related personnel
Data collection strategy: Questionnaire/survey

1.4 Special education teachers perceive participation in the program as positive and effective.
Data source: Special education teachers/related personnel
Data collection strategy: Questionnaire/survey

Standard 2

Quality special education programs involve all personnel who work with handicapped students in appropriate training to strengthen their ability to provide effective services.

2.1 All personnel who work with handicapped students attend relevant in-service training sessions during the academic year.
Data source: Teachers/related personnel
Data collection strategy: Survey

2.2 Topics offered for in-service training sessions are identified on the basis of the school's specific program needs.
Data source: Teachers/related personnel
Data collection strategy: Survey

2.3 Topics offered for in-service training sessions are identified on the basis of the school's specific program needs.
Data source: Staff development records/principal
Data collection strategy: Checklist/survey

Standard 3

Facilities provided for educating handicapped students maximize integration of handicapped students within the total school environment in ways that go beyond minimal legal compliance.

3.1 Special education classrooms are located centrally within the mainstream environment.
Data source: Special education classrooms/principal/teachers/related personnel
Data collection strategy: Observation/questionnaire

3.2 Portable or mobile classrooms are utilized only when regular education classes for students of similar chronological age also are housed in such settings.
Data source: Special education classrooms/principal/teachers/related personnel
Data collection strategy: Observation/questionnaire

Standard 4

The range and variety of instructional materials, supplies, and equipment for the special education program are sufficient to meet effectively the needs of students served.

4.1 Materials, equipment, and supplies that are appropriate to a variety of learning styles and learner characteristics are available in each special education classroom.
Data source: Special education teachers/special education classrooms
Data collection strategy: Questionnaire/survey/observation

4.2 Sufficient materials, supplies, and equipment suitable for the range of ability levels found in each special education class are available for all instructional domains addressed in the setting.
Data source: Special education teachers/special education classrooms
Data collection strategy: Questionnaire/survey/observation

4.3 Materials, supplies, and equipment for the special education program are current and in good repair.
Data source: Special education classrooms
Data collection strategy: Observation

4.4 Teachers, paraprofessionals, diagnostic personnel, and related service personnel have ready access to necessary materials/equipment.
Data source: Special education teachers/related personnel
Data collection strategy: Survey/checklist

Standard 5

Quality special education programs exceed minimal compliance standards with respect to implementing procedures to identify and place those in need of special education services.

5.1 All state and federal regulations and guidelines pertaining to the referral, screening, and placement process are carried out effectively, efficiently, and in a timely manner.
Data source: Placement forms/IEPs
Data collection strategy: Checklist

5.2 Ample consultative services are available to assist regular class teachers during prereferral intervention efforts.
Data source: Teachers
Data collection strategy: Questionnaire/survey

5.3 School personnel actively encourage parent participation and effectively communicate program goals and options to parents.
Data source: Parents/related school personnel
Data collection strategy: Questionnaire/survey

Standard 6

Quality programs for handicapped students exceed minimal compliance standards with respect to maximizing students' participation in the regular education program with nonhandicapped peers.

6.1 Students have access to a full array of service-delivery options representing varying degrees of integration with mainstream programs, including, at the high school level, work-study and vocational options.
Data source: Teachers/students/parents
Data collection strategy: Questionnaire/survey/checklist

6.2 School personnel make every effort to serve exceptional students in the least restrictive setting possible.
Data source: Teachers/students/parents/special education classrooms/ IEP documents
Data collection strategy: Questionnaire/survey/standardized instrument/checklist

Standard 7

Effective special education programs are well coordinated.

7.1 Key school personnel with whom each special education student comes in contact systematically monitor his or her progress.
Data source: Teachers/related personnel
Data collection strategy: Survey/questionnaire/checklist

7.2 School-based services are coordinated with other social services.
Data source: Parents
Data collection strategy: Survey/questionnaire/checklist

7.3 There is ongoing communication between school and home.
Data source: Students' permanent records/parents
Data collection strategy: Survey/questionnaire

Standard 8

Students are successful in the special education program.

8.1 Students and their parents perceive students' participation in the program as positive.
Data source: Students/parents
Data collection strategy: Survey/questionnaire

8.2 Students and/or their parents are satisfied with students' progress.
Data source: Parents/students
Data collection strategy: Survey/questionnaire

Standard 9

Quality special education programs implement program evaluation activities that go beyond those required for purposes of compliance monitoring.

9.1 Outcomes addressing the academic, vocational, life skills, and transition elements of the special education program are evaluated routinely.
Data source: IEPs/annual program reports/principal
Data collection strategy: Checklist/survey/questionnaire

9.2 Program resources are evaluated routinely.
Data source: IEPs/annual program reports/principal
Data collection strategy: Checklist/survey/questionnaire

9.3 Program processes such as identification, placement and exiting procedures, program organization, instructional methods, and curriculum content are evaluated routinely.
Data source: IEPs/annual program reports/principal
Data collection strategy: Checklist/survey/questionnaire

Standard 10

Quality special education programs emphasize principles of effective practice widely held to be applicable across grade levels and areas of exceptionality.

10.1 The daily instructional program provided for each special education student derives from his or her IEP.
Data source: Teachers' plan book/IEPs/special education classrooms
Data collection strategy: Checklist/observation

10.2 A variety of presentation modes and materials are utilized routinely in instruction, including those not commonly used in mainstream classes.
Data source: Special education classrooms/special education teachers
Data collection strategy: Observation/checklist

10.3 Direct instruction and mastery learning techniques are employed, with students' progress monitored and recorded in an ongoing fashion.
Data source: Teachers' plan book/special education classrooms
Data collection strategy: Checklist/observation

10.4 Systematic instructional sequences that support transfer and generalization of newly learned skills are provided.
Data source: Instructional product portfolio/special education classrooms
Data collection strategy: Checklist/observation

10.5 Classrooms are characterized by high rates of student time on task.
Data source: Special education classrooms
Data collection strategy: Observation

10.6 Multiple strategies to motivate students are utilized, including such things as verbal praise, use of high-interest materials, contingency contracting, and the communication of positive regard for students.
Data source: Special education classrooms
Data collection strategy: Checklist/observation

10.7 Special education teachers routinely follow students' progress and monitor their performance in mainstream classes.
Data source: Student records/teachers
Data collection strategy: Checklist/questionnaire

Standard 11

In addition to reflecting principles of sound practice that apply across special education programs (see Standard 10), quality programs for exceptional students at the secondary level also reflect principles widely held to be applicable to the secondary level.

11.1 Transition objectives and plans are incorporated in IEPs at the secondary level.
Data source: IEPs/special education teachers
Data collection strategy: Checklist/survey/questionnaire

11.2 Secondary special education programs include collaboration with appropriate adult service agencies.
Data source: IEPs/special education teachers
Data collection strategy: Checklist/survey/questionnaire

11.3 The vocational curriculum for secondary special education students includes opportunities for community-based instruction and actual job experience.
Data source: Teachers/related personnel
Data collection strategy: Survey/questionnaire

11.4 Secondary special education students participate in instruction in independent living skills.
Data source: IEPs/special education teachers
Data collection strategy: Survey/questionnaire

Standard 12

In addition to reflecting those general practices that apply across special education programs (see Standard 10), quality programs for severely and profoundly handicapped (S/PMH) children reflect principles of sound practice widely held to be appropriate for this population.

12.1 Functional assessment (i.e., assessment that goes beyond standardized testing and includes use of criterion-referenced methods of observing behavior as well as frequency, duration, and time sampling of behavior) in educational, psychological, motor, sensory, and communication areas is conducted for each S/PMH student.
Data source: IEPs/special education teachers/related personnel
Data collection strategy: Checklist/survey/questionnaire

12.2 Assessment includes consideration of places and settings beyond the school classroom where the S/PMH student functions.
Data source: IEPs/special education teachers/related personnel
Data collection strategy: Checklist/survey/questionnaire

12.3 A functional curriculum is stressed whereby instruction focuses on developing skills that are of the highest priority for S/PMH students in their school, home, community, and potential vocational environments.
Data source: IEPs/special education teachers/related personnel/ special education classrooms
Data collection strategy: Checklist/survey/observation

12.4 The major curriculum domains for S/PMH students include development of domestic, leisure/recreation, vocational, and community skills.
Data source: IEPs/special education teachers/related personnel/ special education classrooms
Data collection strategy: Checklist/survey/observation

12.5 Assessment and instruction of S/PMH students occur in natural settings, such as the home and community, as well as in classroom settings.

Data source: IEPs/special education teachers/related personnel
Data collection strategy: Checklist/survey/questionnaire

Standard 13

The climate for special education reflects a sense of belonging among students and staff. Students and staff members feel they are a part of the total school environment.

13.1 School personnel make every effort to integrate special education students along social, academic, and temporal dimensions to the greatest extent possible.

Data source: Students/school personnel/parents/placement meetings
Data collection strategy: Questionnaire/survey/observation

13.2 Special education students and staff participate in a full range of school processes (e.g., extracurricular activities and duty assignments).

Data source: Students/school personnel/parents
Data collection strategy: Questionnaire/survey

Standard 14

School personnel hold positive attitudes toward handicapped students and work to promote educational growth and development of positive self-concepts among these children.

14.1 Regular class teachers readily make accommodations in their classes to integrate handicapped students.

Data source: Students/school personnel/parents/regular classes
Data collection strategy: Questionnaire/survey/observation

14.2 Administrators support mainstreaming efforts and assist teachers in reaching this goal.

Data source: Students/school personnel/parents
Data collection strategy: Questionnaire/survey

14.3 School personnel expect handicapped students to be successful.

Data source: Students/school personnel/parents
Data collection strategy: Questionnaire/survey

Resource B:
Selected References

The following articles may serve as general resources on the topic of program evaluation and special education.

Austin, G. R. (1979). Exemplary schools and the search for effectiveness. *Educational Leadership, 27,* 10-14.
Bickel, W. E., & Bickel, D. D. (1986). Effective schools, classrooms, and instruction: Implications for special education. *Exceptional Children, 52,* 489-500.
Haertel, G., Katzenmeyer, C., & Haertel, E. (1988, March). *Capturing the quality of schools: Approaches to evaluation.* Paper presented at annual meeting of the American Educational Research Association, San Francisco.
Stevens, R., & Rosenshine, B. (1981). Advances in research on teaching. *Exceptional Education Quarterly, 2*(1), 1-9.
Ysseldyke, J. E., & Mirkin, P. K. (1981). The use of assessment information to plan instructional interventions: A review of the research. In C. Reynolds & T. Gutkin (Eds.), *A handbook for school psychology* (pp. 295-410). New York: John Wiley.
Ysseldyke, J. E., & Shinn, M. R. (1981). Psychoeducational evaluation. In J. M. Kauffman & D. P. Hallahan (Eds.), *The handbook of special education* (pp. 418-440). Englewood Cliffs, NJ: Prentice-Hall.
Zigmond, N., & Miller, S. E. (1986). Assessment for instructional planning. *Exceptional Children, 52,* 501-510.
Zigmond, N., Silverman, R., & Laurie, T. (1978). Competencies for teachers of secondary students with learning disabilities. In L. Mann, L. Goodman, & J. L. Weiderholt (Eds.), *Teaching the learning disabled adolescent* (pp. 279-292). Boston: Houghton Mifflin.
Zigmond, N., Vallecorsa, A., & Silverman, R. (1981). *Assessment for instructional planning in special education.* Englewood Cliffs, NJ: Prentice-Hall.

The articles that follow illustrate alternative data-collecting techniques for the evaluation of special education programs.

Carter, J., & Sugai, G. (1989). Survey of preferral practices: Responses from state departments of education. *Exceptional Children, 55,* 298-302. (survey)

Deno, S. L., & Fuchs, L. S. (1988). Developing curriculum-based measurement systems for data-based special education problem solving. In E. L. Meyen, G. A. Vergason, & R. L. Whelan (Eds.), *Effective instructional strategies* (pp. 481-504). Denver, CO: Love. (informal assessment techniques)

Hasazi, S. B., Gordon, L. R., & Roe, C. A. (1985). Factors associated with the employment status of handicapped youth exiting high school from 1979 to 1983. *Exceptional Children, 51,* 455-469. (interview)

Helton, G. B. (1988). Guidelines for assessment in special education. In E. L. Meyen, G. A. Vergason, & R. J. Whelan (Eds.), *Effective instructional strategies for exceptional children* (pp. 391-414). Denver, CO: Love. (general assessment decisions)

Leinhardt, G., & Seewald, A. M. (1980). *Student-Level Observation of Beginning Reading manual.* Pittsburgh, PA: Learning Research and Development Center, University of Pittsburgh. (observational system)

Leindhardt, G., Zigmond, N., & Cosley, W. W. (1981). Reading instruction and its effects. *American Educational Research Journal, 18,* 343-362. (observation system)

Mithaugh, P., Horiuchi, C., & Fanning, P. (1985). A report on the Colorado statewide follow-up survey of special education students. *Exceptional Children, 51,* 397-404. (survey)

The sources that follow provide program standards for special education. The standards often have been developed by national and state agencies.

Council for Exceptional Children. (1983). Code of ethics and standards for professional practice. *Exceptional Children, 50,* 205-210.

Council of Administrators of Special Education. (1985). *Research committee information packet: Critical success factors of special education administrators.* Reston, VA: Council for Exceptional Children.

Delaware State Education Agency. (1984). *Program standards for special education and related services: Levels I-IV and Level V.* Dover: Author.

Kentucky State Department of Education. (1985). *Kentucky SE independent living: A special education supplement for the Kentucky standards for grading, classifying and accrediting schools.* Lexington: Author.

National RRC Panel on Indicators of Effectiveness in Special Education. (1986). *Effectiveness indicators for special education.* Hampton, NH: Center for Resource Management.

Roddy, E. A. (1984). *The quest for quality in special education: Defining significant variables.* Concord, NH: Task Force for the Improvement of Secondary Special Education in New Hampshire.

Schrag, J. A. (1987). Implementation of P.L. 94-142 and its accomplishments, problems and future challenges: A state education agency perspective. In H. J. Prehm (Ed.), *The future of special education* (pp. 75-110). Reston, VA: Council for Exceptional Children.

Vermont Department of Education. (1985). *Special education quality indicator manual*. Burlington: Author.

Virginia State Department of Education, Division of Special Education Programs. (1989). *Handbook to guide development of programs for severely and profoundly handicapped students*. Richmond: Author.

Warger, C. L., & Weiner, B. B. (Eds.). (1987). *Secondary special education: A guide to promising public school programs*. Reston, VA: Council for Exceptional Children.

The following references serve as a general guide to special education programming. Many of the following references are considered basic texts for special educators.

Asch, A. (1989). Has the law made a difference? What some disabled students have to say. In D. Lipsky & A. Gartner (Eds.), *Beyond separate education: Quality education for all* (pp. 181-205). Baltimore: Brookes.

Bricker, D. D. (1984). An analysis of early intervention programs: Attendance issues and future directions. In P. J. Morris & B. Blatt (Eds.), *Special education: Research and trends* (pp. 28-65). New York: Pergamon.

Deshler, D., & Schumaker, J. (1986). Learning strategies: An instructional alternative for low-achieving adolescents. *Exceptional Children, 52*, 583-590.

Hahn, H. (1989). The politics of special education. In D. Lipsky & A. Gartner (Eds.), *Beyond separate education: Quality education for all* (pp. 225-241). Baltimore: Brookes.

Hallahan, D. P., & Kauffman, J. M. (1991). *Exceptional children: Introduction to special education* (5th ed.). Englewood Cliffs, NJ: Prentice-Hall.

Heward, W., & Orlansky, M. (1991). *Exceptional children* (4th ed.). Columbus, OH: Charles E. Merrill.

Idol, L. (1988). A rationale and guidelines for establishing special education consultation programs. *Remedial and Special Education, 9*, 48-58.

Kauffman, J., Gerber, M., & Semmel, M. (1988). Arguable assumptions underlying the regular education initiative. *Journal of Learning Disabilities, 21*, 6-12.

Marozas, D. S., & May, D. C. (1988). *Issues and practices in special education*. New York: Longman.

Masters, L. F., & Mori, A. A. (1986). *Teaching secondary students with mild learning and behavior problems*. Rockville, MD: Aspen Systems.

Mayer, C. L. (1982). *Educational administration and special education: A handbook for school administrators*. Boston: Allyn & Bacon.

McDaniel, E. A., Sullivan, P. D., & Goldbaum, J. L. (1982). Physical proximity of special education classrooms to regular classrooms. *Exceptional Children, 49*, 73-75.

Mercer, C. D., & Mercer, A. R. (1988). *Teaching children with learning problems* (3rd ed.). Columbus, OH: Charles E. Merrill.

Meyen, E. L., Vergason, G. A., & Whelan, R. J. (Eds.). (1988). *Effective instructional strategies for exceptional children*. Denver, CO: Love.

Noonan, M. J., & Hemphill, N. J. (1988). Comprehensive curricula for integrating severely disabled and nondisabled students. In E. L.

Meyen, G. A. Vergason, & R. J. Whelan (Eds.), *Effective instructional strategies for exceptional children* (pp. 157-172). Denver, CO: Love.

Point, C., Zins, J., & Graden, J. (1988). Implementing a consultation-based service delivery system to decrease referrals for special education: A case study of organizational considerations. *School Psychology Review, 17,* 89-100.

Polloway, E. A., Payne, J. S., Patton, J. R., & Payne, R. A. (1985). *Strategies for teaching retarded and special needs children* (4th ed.). Columbus, OH: Charles E. Merrill.

Wang, M., Reynolds, M., & Walberg, H. (Eds.). (1987). *Handbook of special education: Research and practice* (Vol. 1). New York: Pergamon.

Ysseldyke, J. E., & Algozzine B. (1990). *Introduction to special education* (2nd ed.). Boston: Houghton-Mifflin.

The following sources are materials distributed by the U.S. Department of Education that may prove helpful in understanding special education programs.

U.S. Department of Education. (1988). *Tenth annual report to Congress on implementation of the education of the Handicapped Act.* Washington, DC: Government Printing Office.

U.S. Department of Education. (1989). *Eleventh annual report to Congress on implementation of the education of the Handicapped Act.* Washington, DC: Government Printing Office.

U.S. Department of Education. (1990). *Twelfth annual report to Congress on implementation of the education of the Handicapped Act.* Washington, DC: Government Printing Office.

U.S. Department of Education, Office of Educational Research and Improvement. (1986). *The search for successful secondary schools: The first three years of the secondary school recognition program.* Washington, DC: Government Printing Office.

U.S. Office of Education. (1977). Education of handicapped children: Implementing of Part B of the Education of the Handicapped Act. *Federal Register 42,* 42474-42518.

U.S. Office of Education. (1977). Regulations for implementing Section 504 of the Rehabilitation Act of 1973. *Federal Register 42,* 22677-22685.

The references below refer to instruments illustrated in two of the vignettes and also include a computer program described in a third vignette.

Rafferty, J., Norlina, R., Tamaru, R., McMath, C., & Morganstein, D. (1985). *Statworks*. Philadelphia: Cricket Software.

Ysseldyke, J. E., & Christenson, S. L. (1987). *The Instructional Environment Scale.* Austin, TX: Pro-Ed.

Index

American Educational Research Association, 97
Attention deficit-hyperactivity disorder (ADHD), 12

Behavior, on-task: of students, 54, 55, 66, 67
Behavior records, coded, 56-57

Classroom activity, direct observation of, 55
Classrooms: activity in, 52-70; needed improvements in, 52-54
Community relations programs, evaluation of, vii
Counseling programs, evaluation of, vii

Data collection, 42-43; summarizing results of, 66-67
Data collection methods, 18-19, 38, 50, 85; alternatives strategies of, 6-7, 19, 39, 51, 69, 81, 95; articles illustrating alternative, 105-106; checklists, 9, 74, 75-79, 81-82, 85, 86, 87, 88-89, 90, 95; confidentiality in, 18, 38, 50, 69, 81; direct observation, 9, 74; document reviews, 9; formative evaluation questions, 42; for school program evaluation, 6, 8, 9; group meetings, 51; interviews, 51, 81; needs assessments, 9; parent conferences, 89-91; questionnaires, 9, 13-14, 43-44, 45-46, 47, 51, 85, 95; review of teachers' planning books, 81; seeking redundant information, 19, 51; selection of, 18, 38, 50, 54, 68, 81, 94; specificity in, 19; standardized instruments, 9; summative evaluation questions, 42-43; surveys, 9, 85, 95; telephone surveys, 51, 95
Data summary forms, 64; student, 65
Disabilities, children with, 83

Education of All Handicapped Children Act, 1, 20
Evaluation, school program: and documenting needs, 2, 4; and identifying alternatives, 4; and improving school curricula, vii; and summarization of data, 14, 16-18; and supporting requests for additional resources, 2, 4; as essential tool for school personnel, 1, 4; available resources for, 6; conducting, viii, 4, 6; designing, viii, 6, 50, 81; feasibility of conducting, viii; focusing, viii, 6, 13, 18, 38, 41-42, 50, 68, 73, 81, 84-85, 94; formative, 86; general resources on, 105; interpreting results of, viii, 16, 19, 37-38, 47-48, 51, 67, 70, 79-80, 82, 95; managing, 6; planning, 6, 9-10, 50; principles of, 6; reasons for, 1-3, 8-9; results of, 6, 14, 36-37, 44, 47, 63, 66, 76-77, 78-79, 89-91; selecting

method for analyzing data for, 6; selecting staff for, 8; specifying purposes of, 6; structuring, viii; time frame for, 6; utilizing results of, viii, 16-18, 38, 49-50, 67-68, 80, 91, 94; value of to school professionals, vii, 3-4
Evaluation principles, 18-19, 38-39, 50-51, 68-69, 80-81, 94
Evaluation studies, 57

IEPs, 1, 77, 81, 82, 94; and parental involvement, 41, 89; content of, 71-82; development of checklist for review of, 75-77; documents/files of, 75, 76, 79; frequency of transition objectives in, 79; number of transition objectives in, 78; review of, 76; type of transition objectives in, 80; use of checklist to guide review of, 75; use of transition goals/objectives in, 73-74
Individualized educational plans. *See* IEPs
Instruction, effective: components of, 24
Instructional Environment Scale, The. *See* TIES
Instructional materials: and quality special education programs, 99; assessment of, 73
Intervention strategies, self-help, 84

Language arts instructional programs, evaluation of, vii
Learning disabilities, 12
Least Restrictive Environment (LRE) Placements, appropriateness of, 20-39

Mainstreaming, 83; of mildly handicapped students, 23; problems of, 21-22
Mainstreaming movement, 20
Mainstream instructional environment, 21; and quality special education programs, 99, 100; assessment of, 22, 23

Mathematics instructional programs, vii; evaluation of, vii
Mentally handicapped children, severely/profoundly, 84

National Council on Measurement in Education, 97
Naturalistic observation procedures, use of, 85-86

Observation instruments: formal, 56-57; informal, 56; reliability of, 62-63; SOBR system, 57-59
Observation record forms, 69; blank, 60; completed, 61
Observation sampling plan, 68
Observation strategy, alternatives to, 69
Observation systems: and coding systems, 68; development of, 68
Observers: reliability of, 63, 69; training of, 59, 62, 69

Parental involvement, importance of, 41-42
Parent conferences, obtaining information at, 89-91
Personnel development programs, vii; evaluation of, vii
Program evaluation activities, and quality special education programs, 101
Program participants, satisfaction of, 40-51
Public school law, and exceptional children, 19

Reading instructional programs, vii; evaluation of, vii
Regular education initiative. *See* REI
REI, 83-84; concern for integrated service delivery and, 83

School disciplinary programs, evaluation of, vii
School programs: appropriateness of, 1; quality of, 1

Self-help skills observation checklist, 87, 88, 89, 90, 94; administration of, 88-89; field-testing of, 87-89; summaries of results of, 92-93
Skills, generalization of: assessing to other settings, 83-95
SOBR system: behavior categories for, 59; codes for, 58, 59; use of as observation instrument, 57-59
Special education, 20; classrooms, 3; evaluation studies, 10; field of, 1; general resources on, 105; sources of program standards for, 106-107
Special education classes, 69
Special education class time, 70; and total school environment, 104
Special education programming, 72; general guides to, 107-108
Special education programs, vii, 3, 52, 53, 74, 79; design of, 97; evaluation of, vii, 4, 5, 7; external review of, 3; focusing on, 72-73; implementation of, 97; needs of, 4; school-based, 97; standards/indicators of, 5-6, 10, 54, 84, 97-104; success of students in, 101; well-coordinated, 100-101; widely applicable principles of effective practice in, 101-103
Special education services: delivery of, 41; identification of those in need of, 100; placement of those in need of, 100; quality of, 41
Special education students, 79
Special education teachers, 2, 7, 21, 53, 67, 72, 75, 80, 81
S/PMH curriculum guide, 85, 86
Staff development, teacher needs for, 11-19
Staff resources, and quality special education programs, 98
Student assessment programs, evaluation of, vii
Student Observation of Beginning Reading. *See* SOBR
Students: in-class activities of, 69; promotion of positive self-concepts among, 104; with behavior problems, 12. *See also specific categories of students*
Students, at-risk: programs for, vii
Students, exceptional, 70; needs of in mainstream classroom, 16
Students, handicapped, 13, 22
Students, learning disabled (LD), 21; in mainstream classes, 21
Students, mildly handicapped, 4, 20, 21, 23, 55; programs for, 3; teaching academic skills to, 3; teaching social skills to, 3
Students, moderately handicapped, 54, 55
Students, special education, 12; and parental involvement, 41; in mainstreamed classes, 22
Students, special needs, 12
Students, S/PMH, 86, 87, 88; quality special education programs for, 103-104

Teacher training, assessment of, 73
TIES, 22-24, 38; alternatives to use of, 39; data record form of, 30-33; instructional rating form of, 26-29; possible misinterpretations of, 39; scoring results of, 36-37; successful administration of, 24-25, 36; summary/profile sheet of, 34-35
Training, staff in-service: and quality special education programs, 98
Transition goal checklist, 77
Transition objectives, 81, 82; frequency of in IEPs, 79; identification of essential, 74-75; number of, 78

U.S. Department of Education, materials distributed by, 108

Workshops, ideas for in-service, 12-13